Praise for Deborah Flanagan's
BUILDING A POWERFUL PRACTICE

Deborah has written a comprehensive guide which answers the many questions and concerns I have had about creating and nurturing my own practice. With simplicity, candor, warmth, humor, tremendous knowledge and experience, she shares countless insights as well as those of her colleagues to provide a solid and accessible framework that any new practitioner can follow.

—Barbara Becker, Reiki practitioner, Jersey City/NYC

Building a Powerful Practice is a thorough and comprehensive guide to creating and building your own wellness practice. Deborah shares practical and doable marketing and business-building information, and breaks it into manageable chunks. The stories she shares from her experiences, as well as the experiences of other wellness practitioners, add to and clarify the reality of building this type of business. The questions she offers at the end of each chapter help you to define and clarify your own path and help you see there isn't a cookie-cutter, one-size-fits-all approach to creating your business. This book is a wonderful resource if you are just starting your own wellness business, as well as if you're in need of a little extra support and inspiration as you grow your business. Deborah's warmth and knowledge come through in each chapter, and her experience helps demystify the process of where and how to begin.

—Beth Tascione, Yoga teacher and Reiki Master at
Yoga Bliss, Northampton, MA • yogablissnyc.com

This gem of a book contains a plethora of relevant advice, practical actions, and lessons learned to help you establish your successful wellness business in the best way possible for you. Deborah draws from her experience of transitioning from a full time office job to where she is today as founder of Center for True Health, to support your transition in a way that is true to you. She generously shares her best tips for success (and timesaving templates), alongside those of a diverse range of established practitioners, to help you attract your ideal clients and grow your business, while respecting self care, healthy boundaries, and heart-centered business practices.

—Nicola Wardhaugh, Reflexologist at Singers Lane Reflexology,
United Kingdom • singerslanereflexology.com

Like Deborah Flanagan herself, this book is down-to-earth, practical, and clear while still being compassionate, heart-centered, and light. Deborah tells it like it is without preaching a one-size-fits-all approach. She offers a series of questions for practitioners to ask themselves about various aspects of the business side of wellness work while emphasizing the natural evolution of any solo practice.

New and growing practitioners will find specific suggestions and insights on how to start or develop their solopreneur wellness businesses, from the author and various other practitioners who have successfully built and nurtured their own businesses without ever losing their passion or soulful approach to their work. Potential or beginning professional practitioners have plenty of room to keep dreaming while honestly exploring just what it takes to make their dreams of helping others a reality.

In this book, "business" isn't a dirty word; it is both love- and brain-connected. This outlook is sorely needed in the wellness world. I look forward to recommending this book to my own professionally minded students. I picked up ideas and inspirations for myself, as well. Highly recommended.

—Alice Risemberg, Reiki Teacher, Reiki Pulse
Roseville, CA • reikipulse.com

Building a Powerful Practice

Successful Strategies for Your Wellness Business

BUILDING

A

POWERFUL PRACTICE

SUCCESSFUL STRATEGIES FOR YOUR WELLNESS BUSINESS

DEBORAH FLANAGAN

*To all the wonderful teachers, clients, and students
who showed me the way with this work (and
continue to show me), especially Pingo.*

Contents

Acknowledgments

Special thanks to Sarah and Shawn Carson, Joanna Crespo, Pamela Herrick, Maria Rodriguez, Frans Stiene, Gary Strauss, and Melissa Tiers for their insightful feedback and perspectives on how to build a successful practice. Thank you to my students and fellow practitioners for sharing your questions about what you wanted to know as you built your own practice.

Thanks also to Elliott Beard, Tom Conte, Katie Kretschmer, Molly Lindley, and Krista Vossen, who contributed their exceptional expertise and guidance in putting together this book.

Introduction

I wrote this book to help new wellness practitioners create a vibrant, successful practice. Over the past few years, so many new practitioners have asked me to meet for coffee to "pick my brain" because their various trainings didn't fully prepare them for the business side of starting a practice. This book is the product of those coffee dates, but is more comprehensive (with less caffeine!).

So often I hear new, as well as more seasoned, practitioners struggling to make a living doing the work they love. Common questions include: How can I find and keep clients? How do I figure out what to charge? How do I find office space? This book is geared toward wellness practitioners interested in creating their own full or part-time practice, as well as building partnerships with healthcare providers. While it's geared toward practitioners who are just starting out, it can be helpful for anyone who wants to build a thriving practice.

Since my training is in Reiki, hypnosis, and reflexology, I can speak directly to practitioners of these disciplines. I also interview practitioners and teachers of polarity, massage, Thai massage, astrology, and neuro-linguistic programming (NLP). Other kinds of bodywork or coaching also fit well within this rubric.

While I live and practice in New York City, the practitioners I have interviewed for the book live and work internationally, in big cities and small towns and rural communities. I give you suggestions and ideas that you can adapt to where you live and work, and that are easy to personalize depending on your individual needs and circumstances.

As I created my practice from scratch, I spent a lot of time, effort, and angst finding my way and figuring out what business strategies worked best for me. I want to help new practitioners avoid the pitfalls and worry I faced in the beginning, so that you can connect more quickly with the work you love to do: helping people help themselves.

Throughout the book, I address the most common questions I hear from new practitioners. I share what's worked for me, as well as other approaches and perspectives from a variety of wellness practitioners, teachers, and experts. I've also included a Business Starter Kit on my website (centertruehealth.com/business-starter-kit) that will give you templates and resources you can use right away.

What if I don't have a business mind-set?

I hear this from so many practitioners, and I can completely relate. I used to think I wasn't entrepreneurial in any way, shape, or form. Years ago, if you told me I would one day have my own business and that I would really enjoy it, I would never have believed you. (And I would have panicked!) If I can do it, you can do it, and I'm here to show you how.

This book is fundamentally heart-centered, but it also includes a strong focus on practical realities. I include questions to prompt reflection throughout the book, and I encourage you to answer them as you read to help you figure out what's important to you, and what your priorities are, as you create your practice. Having a business mind-set is something that can be learned, and that's what this book is all about: giving you a clear roadmap on how to set up your practice in a way that works for you, so that you can really enjoy doing the work you love.

For me, the most important thing I learned about creating my own business was that it doesn't have to conflict with the values most wellness practitioners share: helping others and doing good work in the world. Business can be about being heart-centered and connecting with people. In fact, I think this sincerity and integrity comes through in the way you do your work, and your clients will value and recognize the difference. Reminding myself often of this truth helped me trust the process of creating and running my own practice.

Okay, but how do I even start building a business?

Right off the bat I want to acknowledge something: you're going to feel a little scared or worried or overwhelmed when you start out. I'd venture to say this is true of any new endeavor that stretches you and helps you grow. I definitely experienced all these emotions at different stages in my practice (and continue to experience them as I expand into new avenues of growth). But step by step, the recommendations I outline in this book will help you make a more seamless transition to your new career.

Leaping into your own full-time wellness practice can be scary, but the sooner you begin, the sooner you'll be on your way. In contrast, one extremely gifted practitioner who I met in my reflexology program is still worrying about what kind of massage table to get, and we finished our program seven years ago. You just have to jump in and get started. Doing a little bit every day and finding a way to stay centered is the way to go. Be gentle with yourself: the growing pains you'll feel throughout the process are normal.

So let's get down to business (pun intended)!

1

Becoming a Professional Practitioner

The most important piece of advice I can give you about making a career transition toward a healing arts practice is this: don't give up your day job! At least initially, keeping your full-time job and then transitioning to a part-time job, or "bridge" job, is best.

What's a bridge job? A bridge job is a temporary position that you take as you leave traditional employment to become a small business owner. In other words, you take a temporary job while you build your business. It can be incredibly stressful to rely solely on client income when you're first starting out as a practitioner. If you have an additional income source—either freelance or part-time work—this can help you be more financially stable as you build your practice. From the beginning, this was really important for me, because I knew I would worry if I didn't have enough clients in a particular week, and I didn't want to worry at the expense of focusing on the work I was doing to help my existing clients.

In my previous career, I was a development director at various arts nonprofits for fifteen years. When I decided to become a wellness practitioner, I first found a part-time job as a fundraising consultant at a holistic education center. This gave me time to get my practice set up and begin to build my client base while still earning a stable income.

At first, any money I earned from clients was extra, and I set it aside as savings to have when I made the transition to a full-time practice.

For me, easing into this career transition was absolutely the best approach, and it created a financial cushion to land on when I finally left my part-time fundraising job. There's no way I could have quit my previous job and started seeing clients full-time—I wouldn't have been able to make a viable living.

I would even go so far as to say you should *always* keep your wellness practice part time, if possible. Do something else, wellness-related or not, just so you're not only seeing clients full-time, which could lead to burnout. Treatment hours are very different than working full-time at an office. With this work, you need to be very present for your clients, and it can be taxing emotionally and physically. I remember when I was first starting out I thought I would be able to see clients for thirty hours a week. Fifteen to twenty hours a week is full-time in terms of treatment hours. Seeing clients full-time is tough, and if you do choose this path, it's all the more important that you take time to take care of yourself and have a strong meditation practice. (I go over my best tips for self-care later in the book.)

Once I stopped consulting, in addition to offering client sessions, I started teaching Reiki classes. Maybe you'll decide to teach, offering workshops or classes, or maybe you want to find ways to make passive income by selling products or something else. Passive income is money you earn when you're not actively working. When you do a client session you get paid a set fee for an hour of your time; when you sell a product—for example, a bottle of essential oil or a recording—you're getting paid without having to be physically present to offer a service.

Or maybe you'll find a part-time job you enjoy to supplement your income, as discussed above. Working by the hour limits your income potential and it's nice to have a cushion, since client income ebbs and flows depending on the time of year, the state of the economy, the weather, etc. These are important issues to consider as you're starting out.

Other ways of making the switch

Of course, every practitioner's career transition looks a little different. Polarity teacher and long-time practitioner Gary Strauss earned his master's degree in nutrition and began his career as a researcher in a New York City hospital.

"The hospital was part of my journey along the way. Once I got clear that I wanted to be able to do this work [Polarity], I did everything I could to build a practice. I worked on people all the time and I took classes with really great practitioners to model them.

"Since I was working at the hospital, I didn't have pressure to have to make a living from my Polarity work. I knew one day it would take care of me, but it developed very slowly, and I always had other jobs to balance my life financially.

"It was never about what I was doing, it was always about being balanced and happy in the moment with what I had—in other words, enjoying the process and journey along the way. I worked in any way that I could with Polarity and followed every possibility or lead. I still do this."

Integrative hypnosis practitioner and trainer Melissa Tiers gradually transitioned into her work:

"I was a rock and roll musician for most of my life and hypnosis was a hobby. I've always been fascinated by altered states of consciousness— from spinning and hyperventilating when I was five years old to psychedelics in my teens. Once I got a glimpse of the malleability of mind and perception, I never stopped searching for the boundaries of what was possible. I'm smiling as I remember all the aha moments sprinkled throughout this time. I used to go to science of consciousness conventions looking for answers and what I got was even better: more questions. I started exploring bizarre altered states at The Monroe Institute and the aha's got bigger.

"I would hypnotize people in the dressing room of CBGB's and was able to experiment with all kinds of hypnotic phenomena. I would read Milton Erickson's work and play with anyone who would let me. It was so interesting that I started doing it part time. I mean let's face it, being a musician in New York City hardly paid the rent. It was fun, but hypnosis was better.

"I started to see more and more people and was constantly amazed and humbled by what people were capable of changing. I went to a weekend hypnosis training and got hooked. I went to another and another, and well, I never stopped."

Hypnosis and NLP trainers and practitioners Sarah and Shawn Carson made their career transition quite differently, as Sarah explains:

"I think our path may be rather different than many, as we decided to take two years off from our jobs to pursue our dreams.

"One of Shawn's interests was NLP—he had heard about it many years before, but never had the opportunity to study. His interest led to studying hypnosis and to my interest. Having completed our NLP training and hypnosis training we started to see clients. Shawn continued his business consulting on a part-time basis, and still does.

"We started out part time, and when we first began it was just an occasional client, however, this changed pretty quickly as we began to teach NLP/hypnosis and made the decision to set up a school here in New York."

Balancing family commitments

Another important consideration is allowing time for family commitments. Reiki teacher and practitioner Joanna Crespo has a full-time job in finance and three kids, and explains how she balances everything:

"It's definitely a balancing act between love and guilt. I am fortunate to have a husband who believes a happy wife is a happy family, and he often helps out [with their children] during the weekends when I'm teaching or seeing clients. To compensate for my busy schedule, I make an effort to openly share myself with my family so they know we are always together in love. My health or having enough rest is an ongoing concern."

Thai massage therapist and coach Pamela Herrick has an eight-year-old son, and talks about how she learned to manage a full-time practice despite major changes in her personal life:

"Having a private practice and working solo has been a perfect fit for me professionally, and for my family. When my son was very young, I limited my hours, worked when my husband didn't, and rarely needed a babysitter.

"When my husband and I divorced, we managed to work and take care of our little guy pretty much as we had done when married. Since my son began school, I have been able to see my full roster of clients during school hours, and am able to meet him off the school bus each day, which is a personal priority.

"My son's toddler years were the most difficult. I was breastfeeding, family bedding, and more exhausted than I even knew. When my son started nursery school, I began to see how depleted I was. It was a slow build back, but my clients and my work were one of the most positive parts of myself. My work kept me grounded while I navigated the unfamiliar terrain of mothering."

As you can see, there are many different ways of making a career transition. Hopefully, these stories give you a sense of the possibilities as you move forward in creating a vibrant practice that works with your individual needs and priorities. In the next chapter, I'll home in on specific questions for you to consider regarding the number of client sessions you can offer in a week, depending on what you want your schedule and work flow to look like.

2

Client Hours: What's Realistic

When I was first starting out with my practice, I thought I could do thirty hours of client sessions in a week. Turns out, that's way too many! Not only could I not keep a pace like that now, when I was first starting out, I could do even fewer sessions, because you build up stamina to do this work. In the beginning, if I did three sessions back-to-back, I got tired.

At this stage in my practice, I can comfortably do fifteen to twenty hours of client sessions a week. This number will vary from practitioner to practitioner; I know some practitioners who can do three sessions a day, and one who can do ten. He is definitely the exception—he's an extremely advanced practitioner and teacher, and he also takes a lot of time off. In other words, he's not doing this five days a week, every week.

As I mentioned above, because I had a part-time job as a fundraising consultant when I started my practice, I would see clients starting around 3 p.m. until 9 or 9:30 at night. This made for very long days, and as a result, I was exhausted. Plus, I'm not a night owl—I'm a morning person. While I was very clear with myself that I didn't want to see clients on weekends—I really wanted to reserve that time for myself and for spending time with my husband—it took me a long time to understand that doing client sessions in the late evening didn't work well for me.

After seeing clients for late-evening appointments for a couple years, I gradually began to end my last session of the day earlier. At first, I changed it to end at 7:30 p.m., after a year of that, I started ending at 7:00. Currently, I end at 7 p.m. a couple of nights a week and 6:30 p.m. on other nights.

With new clients, this was easy—they didn't know any different, so the new time boundary was fine with them. It was more difficult with clients who were used to later appointments. But really, once I was truly comfortable with the new time boundary of ending at 7 p.m., they didn't challenge me (or if they did, it didn't bother me). I always remind myself that I'm not the only practitioner out there—there are others who see clients later, and might be a better fit for people who need late appointments.

Gary Strauss explains it this way:

"The issue is that you are creating something that needs to be nurtured under the right sunlight, moisture, and space. Allowing your practice to be open in the beginning, without too much pressure from the outside world as you create it in a life-enhancing way, is best.

"I see too many practitioners burn themselves out based on thirty sessions a week. Why not be in it for the long haul, and give yourself the chance to develop the practitioner skills necessary to be able to sustain a long and healthy career? In the beginning that should mean two to three sessions a day."

Reiki teacher and practitioner Frans Stiene agrees, and writes about the importance of having a personal meditation practice. "In the beginning you might just want to do a few sessions in a day, like three one-hour sessions, for example. However, when you keep doing your own personal practice (within the system of Reiki, or whatever your personal meditation practice includes), you might be able to do eight one-hour sessions in a day, and after that you will feel fantastic. So the key to it is really your own personal practice."

Here is how Joanna Crespo manages her client sessions while holding a full-time office job:

"I schedule clients when I'm not teaching classes on the weekend. Since I see clients at home, I have the luxury to schedule a session for 1.5 hours to 3 hours depending on the client's needs. I generally see clients on Saturday and Sunday between 10 a.m. and 2 p.m.

"I sometimes add appointments outside of my normal schedule for last-minute requests. There are also weekends that I will keep private for myself and family functions."

Pamela Herrick's session hours have evolved over time.

"When I opened my private practice, I saw fifteen to eighteen clients each week—most for one-hour sessions, a few for ninety minutes. At that time, I was still offering 'regular' massage, and Thai massage was a growing aspect of my work.

"As my practice and I have matured together, I have made many adjustments to how I work, how much I work, and when I work. Now I offer treatments ranging in length from 30 minutes to two-and-a-half hours. I work about ten hours a week, and I see clients on weekdays, keeping weekends for family.

"Have I worried each time I have changed the parameters of my work with clients? Yes, I have. But I always made changes when I knew, from a business point of view, that my practice was vibrant enough to justify it.

"After twelve years in the field, I have learned that there will never be enough of me to go around. So I decide how much to work, and how much to charge for my work, based on my own health and the demands of my local market.

"Because Thai massage is physically demanding, and I'm now in my fifties, I am creating online courses for Thai massage therapists based on my experiences managing a private practice over fifteen years. My web-based teaching is a strategic way for me to supplement my income and continue doing the work I love." (Refer to the Business Starter Kit on my website to find out more about this.)

Homework: Figuring out your client hours

Now that you have a sense of how other practitioners have structured their practices, and their recommendations for new practitioners, consider these questions to help you find out what works for you in terms of your schedule:

+ How many clients would you like to see a day? A week?
+ Do you like seeing clients back-to-back?
+ How much of a break do you need during the day?
+ How much time do you spend on administrative, financial, and marketing tasks? (I'll talk more about this in the next chapter.)
+ How much time do you need to take care of yourself?

Again, you won't really know the answers to these questions until you've done it, and done it for some length of time, but this gives you a place to start. As you can see, figuring out the number of hours/ sessions that you can work comfortably is incredibly important. And remember that this number will change over time as you build your stamina and grow as a practitioner.

Also, if you do find yourself overworked, this is a good problem to have, as most new practitioners don't have a full client load when they're just starting out. So the hours you work will evolve for you and you can figure it out over time.

3

Administrative Work: It Takes More Time Than You Think

Building a successful practice involves much more than just the hours you spend seeing clients.

To give you some context, I spend approximately twenty to twenty-five hours a week on administrative work. What do I mean by administrative work? Here are some things that this includes:

- Scheduling appointments with clients
- Answering client questions either before or after sessions, usually by email and sometimes by phone
- Session documentation
- Data entry—how much the client paid, type of payment, etc.
- Budget tracking—totaling how much I earn each month
- Reconciling my business credit card and bank statements
- Writing and formatting my newsletter, twice a month
- Marketing
- Social media posts on Facebook, etc.
- Additional projects—updating my website, creating new classes, writing guest blog posts for other websites, etc.

Transitioning from a full-time job with a set schedule to having my own practice and setting my own schedule was a big adjustment. Managing my schedule is also one of the elements of my practice that's taken me the longest to figure out. Don't worry, though—I'll share my best practices to help you figure out a schedule that works for you. (I'll also go into depth about the various administrative components I mentioned above, so stay tuned.)

My main issue with administrative work is that I always thought it shouldn't take as much time as it takes. I used to try and squeeze it in—five minute here, five minutes there—and would get frustrated at how long it took. It also made me feel scattered.

Now I acknowledge that it takes a fair amount of time to handle all the administrative aspects of my practice. I set aside a designated window at the end of the week to spend on administrative tasks, instead of trying to fit it in here and there. I've also developed a checklist, which helps a lot more than I thought it would. Check out the Business Starter Kit on my website (www.centertruehealth.com/business-starter-kit) for a sample weekly and monthly administrative checklist to help you develop your own list of tasks.

Astrology coach and spiritual counselor Maria Rodriquez puts it this way:

"This is a full-time job, and you have to deal with it the same way you would if you worked in a full-time office job. If you scatter your energies, you'll be exhausted. If you follow a template, you'll be better able to enjoy your work helping clients.

"I set aside a day a week to focus on household tasks and errands, and try not to work on things involving my astrology coaching practice. Of course, sometimes things come up, so you also have to be flexible. You just have to be really clear about what you want to do, and you have to make sure you take a day off somewhere in the midst of everything."

* * *

I wholeheartedly agree. When I first moved into having a full-time practice, I would see clients five days a week. Now I see the same number of clients, but more clients per day, because I realized it works better for me to see more clients on fewer days and have one or two days set aside for administrative work. Fitting in admin work here and there between client sessions made me feel scattered, and not as focused or efficient.

You want to set your schedule up in such a way that you're not running yourself ragged. After all, how can you help take care of others in the work that you do if you're not able to take care of yourself? Because you're supporting yourself through this work, it can be easy to feel guilty if you haven't finished everything you need to do. Believe me, I know! But the truth is, if you make yourself crazy, you're not going to be a good practitioner, and there is always more you can be doing—it's never "done," so you need to find balance along the way.

I also remember what my beautiful Brazilian hairstylist, Ana Paula, told me when I was first starting my practice. She's always booked; she's superpopular because she's amazing at what she does. When I was first starting out in my practice and I told her that I wasn't as busy as I'd like to be seeing clients, she advised me to enjoy the downtime: "Because when you're really busy, you're going to miss the downtime." (And if you live in New York City and have curly hair, definitely check out the Business Starter Kit on my website for her contact information.)

Now I try to appreciate the down time. If clients cancel, or I have a lighter week, I check in with myself to see if I'm feeling tired or need to take care of myself a little more. These times can be a good reminder to think about what you need. It can be hard to trust this feeling, but it's important.

Sometimes I struggle to disconnect from work mode because it's so connected to something I really care about. It's not that I didn't care about my various jobs as a fundraiser—I definitely did—but this is much more personal.

There's also a tendency when you're starting something new to think, "I want to show that I can do this." And perhaps there's also some doubt behind that: "*Can* I do this?" It takes time, so again, be gentle with yourself during the transition as you set up your practice.

Administrative recommendations from other practitioners

The other practitioners I interviewed also spend a similar amount of time on administrative work.

Joanna Crespo: "I spend about fifteen to twenty hours a week on administrative work, which includes marketing, filing, and email correspondence."

Pamela Herrick: "To keep my private practice growing and renewed with new clients, I spend about ten hours a week blogging, maintaining my website, producing workshops, and managing the business of my business. My member site business development gets roughly twenty-five hours a week of my administrative time."

As you can see, if you're doing approximately fifteen client sessions a week, you'll probably be working more than forty hours a week on your practice.

I asked Frans Stiene how he handles the administrative needs of his business. Since Frans constantly travels around the world to teach, I was especially intrigued by his ability to respond to emails from thousands of students, usually within twenty-four hours. Here's what he has to say about how he manages his time so effectively, and his time management tips for new practitioners:

"I think efficient time management comes from working hard as a new practitioner or teacher; it doesn't come easy. Put all your time and effort in it to make it work.

"Personally, I like to respond quickly to emails because if I don't do this, I'll have a huge pile of emails in my in-box and then it takes me much longer to respond. Plus, it might start to overwhelm me if I see so many emails. Therefore, the trick is to answer them as quickly as possible—a done task is done, no need to worry about it.

"Another very important aspect of this is time. The deeper we go within our own personal practice (for me, it's within the system of Reiki), the more we start to let go of the three times: past, present, future. By letting go of the three times, we start to feel we have more time, as we are letting go of the bonds of time.

"We normally feel restricted by time: for example, 'I need to do this before 5 p.m.,' or 'I only have forty-five minutes to do this.' This state of mind creates a bondage, or a limitation; therefore, when we let go of the three times, we start to free ourselves up, which in turn feels like we have all the time in the world."

I love this concept of the three times, and it's something I've been thinking about a lot in my meditation practice as I change the way I think about time. As someone who has always been very good at thinking two weeks into the future, it's good for me to bring myself back to the present moment.

My top three administrative tips

My number-one top administrative tip is to create email templates for frequently asked questions from new and prospective clients. This will save you vast amounts of time and energy. Some examples:

- An intro email giving the details about working with you—your rates, your address, how to book an appointment, etc.
- An email for clients who cancel, asking if they want to reschedule
- An email about how to purchase a gift certificate

My number-two tip is to have a system in place for responding to clients in a timely manner. I try to get back to clients within twenty-four hours. Pamela Herrick sets aside certain times of day to return phone calls and respond to email from clients. "I think phone manners are really important so my clients feel attended to. I want to be fully present with no distractions, for example, in a quiet room vs. driving in the car or walking down the street."

My number-three tip to help you be strategic and efficient with your admin work is to think of the top three tasks you want to accomplish that day. (I find it even more effective if I think about this the night before in preparation.) These should be manageable tasks—not broad goals like "redesign my website," but more bite-size activities like "write the copy for my newsletter," or "reconcile my income and expenses for the month." I've realized that when I don't do this, I spend my time answering emails or doing things that are less important, and then I don't get around to accomplishing my top-priority to-dos.

Stay focused on what you need to do in your practice. You have to create your own discipline when it comes to this kind of work, and this discipline will enable you to better take advantage of the flexibility of having your own business.

Homework: Establishing your administrative routine

Questions to consider:

+ What time of day is best for you to do administrative work?
+ Do you need a separate day to work on administrative tasks?
+ Do you have certain patterns in relation to managing time that you need to change?
+ What are the three things you need to do to get started on your practice for tomorrow? Write them down someplace where you'll see them first thing tomorrow morning.

4

Finding the Right Office Space

A s I was finishing my Reiki training, I started thinking about renting a treatment room. I researched online on websites like Craigslist and I asked my fellow classmates, established practitioners, and my teachers if they knew places where I could rent a treatment room by the hour.

A friend of mine is a Pilates instructor, and she told me about a Pilates studio where she used to teach. The studio included a treatment room next door that I could rent by the hour, and after I looked at a few places, that room was the one I ended up choosing.

I used this space part-time for a couple of years, slowly growing from an hour here or there to renting a half-day. After a year of this, I was able to rent two half-days, and I would rent by the hour as needed for any overflow clients on an additional third day.

Deciding how much time to buy

I recommend renting a room by the hour when you're first starting out. It's the most flexible option, so you don't have to commit to using the treatment space every week at a certain time, which is good if you don't have clients to fill the timeslots. The downside is the treatment space may not be available at exactly the time when your client wants to come; another practitioner sharing the space may reserve it before you do.

To prepare for this, I recommend coming up with some language you can use with clients in advance. Sometimes, when you're addressing an issue that feels hard to discuss, it's often helpful to hear ways others address this kind of situation. For example, "Unfortunately, I don't have any availability that day or time," or "I'm afraid that time doesn't work, but I can offer you this time and day instead."

As your practice progresses, you can expand to a half-day rental. With the half-day rate, you commit to renting the space for the same day and time every week. For example, once I had more clients, I started renting the treatment room every Tuesday from 2 to 9 p.m. The good thing about this is that you know you'll always have the space on the same day and time, and you'll pay a discounted rate compared to hourly rental. The downside is that you may not have enough clients to use the space every Tuesday.

With a full-day rate, you have the space the same day, all day, each week for the month. For example, you'll have access to the space every Tuesday in the month, from 9 a.m. to 9 p.m., which gives you more flexibility to schedule clients, and is cheaper on a per-hour basis than the half-day rate. The risk, of course, is that you may not be able to see enough clients over the course of twelve hours. The hourly rate is the most expensive option because it's the most flexible.

When choosing the option that works for you, start by figuring out the minimum number of clients you need to see, based on your session fees, to cover the cost of the room.

Finding space for a full-time practice

After slowly building my practice and increasing my number of rental days for four years, I was ready to get a full-time space. By this point I was renting three half-days per week, with an additional day rented at the hourly rate as needed. I started looking at new office spaces and found I could rent my own space and have 24/7 access to it for just a little more than I was paying for the Pilates treatment room.

When you suspect that you're at a tipping point, it's a good time to start looking for your own office. Renting my own full-time office definitely felt like a stretch for me. I wasn't sure I could afford it; with the slight increase in rent and the ebb and flow of clients, I would no longer have the flexibility of renting by the hour or half-day depending on client demand.

But there were so many benefits to having my own office: having 24/7 access to it, having a desk in the office where I could do work between sessions, a receptionist, a waiting room, and gaining access to a conference room I could use when teaching Reiki classes. The office I found also had central heat and air conditioning—the old space didn't get much AC and would get quite hot.

To find my own office, once again I started with Craigslist. Some sample search terms to try: "massage office," "holistic office," "therapists," or "massage therapists' space."

I went and looked at several spaces. I liked the idea of being part of a wellness center, but was surprised at how much more expensive many such rentals were. I ended up in a shared office suite, with thirty or so individual offices that housed many different types of businesses (accountants, app developers, a nutritionist, an art therapist, even a French wine merchant named Émile!).

Consider your needs and priorities when finding a space. For example, I like being around other people throughout the day, even if I'm not interacting with them. The treatment room at the Pilates studio was separate from the studio itself. As a result, I didn't come into contact with anyone besides my clients, and that was a little lonely. This kind of one-on-one work is by its nature somewhat isolating, and thinking about your options to be around other people is important.

It's also possible to share with another practitioner. After seeing clients for a year in my own office, I changed my schedule to seeing clients three days a week, and sublet the other two days in my office to an acupuncturist. Again, look on Craigslist or other places where you might find healing arts practitioners, such as holistic education centers, schools where you did your training, any associations you belong to, and so on. Also, send out an email to other wellness practitioners you know, asking them to spread the word to their networks as well.

One additional note: for practitioners in crowded urban areas like New York City, finding space is a much bigger consideration than it is if you live in a smaller city or town. For example, Thai massage therapist Pam Herrick lives in a town of five thousand people, and writes of how her office-space needs have evolved:

"Thai massage is a second career for me. I made a change from working in not-for-profit arts organizations. After completing my training and licensure in massage therapy, I worked briefly in a group practice in order to see how that business was run.

"Within six months, I opened my private practice in a studio at my home (single girl with a mortgage, and it all worked out beautifully!). Eventually I moved to Thailand and cofounded a Thai massage school there with my first husband.

"When I returned to the U.S., I decided to rent space on the main street of a small village. I wanted the feel of a 'shop' as part of a business community. I 'kept shop' there for five years, occasionally with a part-time therapist working with me.

"I have returned to an at-home studio, a purpose-built 'tiny house' on wheels. It's modern and hip, and I love it. Clients walk through my garden, which includes some medicinal Thai herbs, to get to the studio. At fifty, this is how I see my practice being for a good long while."

Working out of your home and making house calls

I know several practitioners who work out of their homes, and this works well for them. Personally, I wanted a stronger boundary between my home and my workspace (and my husband definitely agreed).

If you are planning to work out of your home, there a few things to take into consideration.

You need to have appropriate space in your home. Again, this might be a much bigger consideration if you live in a large city where real estate is at a premium; it doesn't get much smaller than NYC apartments. I know a couple of practitioners who have a dedicated space in their home for sessions. Another practitioner I know transforms her kitchen into her treatment room each day, but I personally don't think that's ideal.

Reiki teacher and practitioner Joanna Crespo talks about how she handles boundaries, and the lessons she learned to make it work best for her:

"When you're doing sessions at home, keep the walkway from the entrance of your home to the session room as neutral as possible. I also keep my session room neutrally decorated so as to not invite personal comments. The lesson I learned when I first started is that clients are not houseguests. There is no need to show them the layout of the house before or after the session. It's completely fine to escort the client to the front door after the session is finished."

Thai massage therapist and coach Pamela Herrick offers this advice:

"I always direct my clients to the treatment space after asking if they need to use the bathroom (which is inside my house—my treatment room is a small building next to the house). All the session work happens in the session room. Don't invite clients into the kitchen for tea, etc. Payment and future booking—everything happens in the treatment space, to keep that boundary clear."

House calls

When I first started out, I made one house call, but it was immediately evident that it wasn't viable for me. The client had a massage table, which made things easier, but she lived a fifty-minute subway ride away. I didn't factor an additional hundred minutes of travel time into my fee!

It was also harder to end the session because I was in her home, and she wanted to chat afterwards. Because I was a new practitioner, it was harder for me to tell her I needed to leave. I did charge a little bit more, but it really didn't make up for the long round-trip commute and the extended session time. I also didn't like the idea of traveling from client to client and prefer seeing clients in my own space.

Some people do like it, though, and if you have a car and appropriately portable equipment it might be something that works well for you. I know a successful long-time reflexologist in New York City who *only* does house calls. Her clientele is older and wealthier—they prefer house calls, and she really enjoys seeing her clients in their homes.

Other options: spas, doctor's offices, hospitals

When I first started out, I considered all my options—including working at spas, in doctor's offices, and in hospital settings—and I recommend you do this, too, so you can determine your work preferences.

I realized that with a spa setting, it's more about people coming to relax, which is really important, but I wanted the opportunity to develop a deeper relationship with my clients, guiding them through major life changes and challenges. With further research, I also learned that that the income from this kind of work, while possibly more steady than having my own practice, was often quite low because the spa takes a large overhead cut and you end up relying largely on tips.

I also worked hard, probably too hard, trying to set up a partnership with my doctor. He was my personal doctor, and he was passionate about integrative medicine, and a big fan of Reiki, hypnosis, and reflexology. However, his office partner was in charge of the operations side of their business, and he wasn't supportive of the idea. We spent a year trying to set something set up, but it ultimately didn't work out.

A couple years later, a client referred me to her neurologist. The neurologist's practice incorporated integrative therapies, and he rented out space to various wellness practitioners. His patients could take advantage of having acupuncture, massage, chiropractic services, and naturopathy all in the same location. The neurologist was excited about being able to offer the modalities I practice to his patients, and offered me space in his large office at a very reasonable rate. He promoted my practice to his patients on his website and in his newsletter, as well as at the office itself. One day I came in and gave free mini-sessions to patients as an introduction.

This partnership ultimately didn't work out either, and I'm not exactly sure why, though I think it might have been because his patients were in the mind-set of having insurance cover their office visits, including integrative therapies such as acupuncture and chiropractic care, and the work I do isn't usually covered by insurance. (As a postscript, the neurologist ended up closing his practice a year later to head up the neurology department at a local hospital. Ultimately, it worked out for the best.)

Even though these partnerships didn't come together, I think they're good examples of potential opportunities that you should pursue with the mind-set that you never know what's going to work out. You need to follow different kinds of leads and see how it goes. It's like looking for a job: you're going to send out lots of applications, go on several interviews, and ultimately take the job that's offered and that is the best fit. Consider an example from my own experience:

As I mentioned, when I began transitioning towards a healing arts career I was a development director at various nonprofits. I'd been setting up informational interviews at places where I thought I might be able to get a part-time job as a fundraising consultant. Specifically, I was looking for organizations that might offer me the opportunity to use my fundraising abilities on behalf of a healthcare organization that incorporated complementary wellness therapies into its programs. This was a topic I felt passionately about, and I knew I would enjoy fundraising for something I believe in.

I was able to secure an informational interview with the development director at NYU Medical Center. I told her I was interested in fundraising for a hospital that incorporated integrative therapies into its existing allopathic medicine model. She told me about the development department at the hospital, and it didn't sound like a fit. At the end of the interview, she mentioned in passing that the hospital had an amazing program offering integrative therapies for women with disabilities.

I was able to arrange an informational interview with the director of *that* program. At first, I was going to volunteer giving Reiki sessions to the patients, but it turned out they had a paid position open for a Reiki practitioner.

I've been with this program since 2010, and have expanded my involvement to include offering Reiki I classes. I don't get paid very much, but I think it adds to my professional credibility to be affiliated with a hospital, and I love the mission of the program. Because the women who participate in the program all have various physical disabilities, they often spend a lot of time in doctors' offices and the hospital. I love being able to offer these women an empowering way to relax and connect with themselves through Reiki, helping them to participate in improving their own health.

My work with NYU Medical Center came about without much effort, and initially it seemed like much more of a long shot than the partnerships with the two doctors I mentioned above. I give you these examples to demonstrate that you never know what's going to work out.

One tip to remember: to make any of these arrangements work, I did need to be gently persistent. I had to follow up several times to get meetings and informational interviews. Follow-up is key: people are busy, and meeting with me wasn't their top priority. For example, make initial contact by phone or email asking for a short fifteen-minute meeting or call, whichever is easier for them. Wait one or two weeks, and if you haven't heard back, gently remind the person that while you understand that they're busy, you're hoping to hear from them at their convenience. If you still haven't heard from them, follow up once more a few weeks later, always being gracious and appreciative.

Homework: Locating the right space for your practice

Questions to consider if you're looking for a work space:

+ Do you want to share with another practitioner or have your own space?
+ What kind of office environment do you want? (Wellness center, practitioners doing similar work, etc.)
+ How do you want to structure your session hours? Do you want to rent space by the hour, or one day a week, etc.?

Questions to consider if you're thinking of doing client sessions from your home:

+ Personal space: Do you feel comfortable having clients ask questions about photos of family members, for example?
+ Time management: Where will clients wait if they arrive early, and how will you handle lingering clients when it's time for them to go?
+ Privacy: If you're sharing the space with family members or roommates, is there sufficient privacy for clients (and vice versa)? Will family or roommates be home while you're doing sessions, and if so, how will you ensure privacy?

Questions to consider if you're thinking of doing house calls:

+ Will you charge more for house calls?
+ Do you have a certain limit to how far you'll travel?
+ Will you require clients to have the appropriate equipment (such as a massage table) or will you bring your own?

5

Home Office: Staying Organized

Whether or not you're seeing clients out of your home, it's important to have a designated space for your administrative work. As a new practitioner, you'll probably rent treatment space part time. As a result, you'll want to create a home office to help you stay organized.

Here are some things you'll need to keep track of:

+ Client files
+ Your own business cards, brochures, and other printed materials
+ Business expense receipts
+ Income and source of that income
+ Tax forms and other accounting paperwork
+ Additional paperwork
+ Office supplies

Unless you have a full-time office, it's important to create some type of workspace at home, to have a dedicated location where you can keep all your files and supplies. According to the IRS, to use the home office as a business expense and an allowable deduction, the area carved out for your home office must be used regularly and exclusively for your business. As I mentioned before, I live in New York City, where space is a precious commodity and apartments are notoriously small. I put a desk in my living room, off to the side, and I keep my files and office supplies in a nearby closet.

You can definitely get creative with this. Years ago, when she was first starting out, my colleague Maria Rodriguez took a closet in her home and outfitted it as a tiny office. She painted it and put up shelves and even built a desk and an actual place to sit in it.

A couple of important basics to note. Legally, you need to keep all client files in a locked filing cabinet to insure client confidentiality. You also want to come up with a good way to keep track of business expense receipts. I have an accordion file folder and keep receipts divided by the expense categories I use for my taxes. For purchases made online, I keep a large running Word document and paste a copy of each receipt into the document (with the most recent receipt at the top of the document.) Careful documentation like this will be helpful for your accountant. According to the IRS, you must retain your tax returns and documentation to support all income and expenses reported on these tax returns. For time requirements to maintain tax records specific to your tax situation and business, refer to www.irs.gov and your state website.

In the Business Starter Kit on my website (www.centertruehealth. com/business-starter-kit) I'll give you a template for tracking your income and expenses in an Excel spreadsheet. Sample tax-deductible business expenses could include:

- Marketing and printing costs (such as business cards and brochures)
- Office supplies
- Credit card fees
- Rent for your office space
- Website design and hosting
- Professional membership fees

Careful tracking of your expenses is so important because having a running understanding of your expenses will prevent you from accidentally outpacing your revenue. The more organized and systematized you can be, the easier it will be to handle the administrative side of your practice. This will give you more time to focus on doing the work you love—seeing clients!

Homework: Setting up your home office

+ Where will you establish an administrative workspace? Do you need it to be private or quiet?
+ Does it have access to everything you need? For example, an Internet connection, place for confidential client files, etc.?
+ Make a prioritized list of any necessary office supplies or furniture you need to purchase such as an accordion file folder for expense receipts, filing cabinet, etc.

6

Defining Your Niche

Before you can dig into the details of how to market your practice and build your client base, which I'll discuss shortly, you'll need to define your ideal client or niche market.

What do I mean by "niche market"? Niche marketing means focusing your marketing efforts on a small, but specific and well-defined segment of the population. In other words, what are the age range, gender, education level, income, background, and presenting issues of your ideal client?

I know it might seem counterintuitive to narrow your focus and get specific about the kinds of clients you want to work with. It's common to hear new practitioners say they want to see anyone and everyone who needs help (I remember thinking this, too), but aiming too broadly actually defuses your ability to attract clients. Here's an analogy: would you go to a restaurant that serves Chinese, Greek, Italian, American, *and* Indian food? Or would you rather go to a restaurant that specializes in one of those?

I remember a story my first Reiki teacher, Margaret Ann Case, told me years ago about finding your niche. She gave the metaphor of a lighthouse shining in the dark. If the lighthouse is moving around, trying to shine brightly for every boat in the ocean, it's not as effective as if the lighthouse is fixed in one place close to shore for the nearby boats who really need the light to navigate near that particular shore.

Now, I'm not saying you can't ever see clients who fall outside your niche, or that you have to have it all figured out before you open your practice. But having some ideas about the kinds of people you'd like to work with will be helpful. For example, back when I was finishing my Reiki III (Reiki Master) training, one of the requirements for certification was to write a business plan. In this business plan I had to define my niche and my ideal client. I came up with some general demographics: I knew I liked working with young professional women aged twenty to thirty-five.

At first I was a little frustrated that I couldn't define my niche more specifically. But looking back, I don't know that I could have narrowed it down further without a process of experimentation in practice. With time, I realized that I really liked working with women dealing with a transition, whether it was a career, relationship, or health issue. These women were ready to make a big change in their lives and do something different, because what they'd been doing wasn't working for them anymore. I wouldn't have been able to know that I liked helping these kind of clients until I worked with enough kinds of people to realize it.

I think if in the beginning you have a general sense of your ideal client, that's a good starting point. And if you're more clear, all the better. Sometimes new practitioners already know exactly what kinds of clients they want to work with, and that's wonderful. For example, I have a colleague who dealt with severe pain in her reproductive system. As a result, she is inspired to help others who are dealing with chronic pain. Similarly, based on your own background, you can bring to the table certain qualities you've learned, or problems you've dealt with or overcome, that you'd like to help other people with—a specific health issue, phobia, or life challenge, for example.

I know another practitioner who comes from the finance sector and really enjoys working with people in this field. He knows firsthand what it feels like to be super-stressed and burned out, looking for something more fulfilling in life. Another colleague is a lawyer, and she focuses her hypnosis practice on helping new lawyers build their confidence in the courtroom. Another practitioner comes from the theater world, and focuses her Reiki practice working with performing artists. These are some examples to give you a range of ideas as you determine your niche. If you have hobbies, expertise, or a certain background or passion for something, this is a great place to start. But it's also okay to simply be as specific as you can, and then let your practice evolve over time like mine did.

Don't be too hard on yourself if you don't know your niche right off the bat, or if your initial ideas about what you want turn out to be misguided. I experimented with different niches early on. I thought maybe I would work with people who have migraines and headaches because of the neurologist I was going to work with. By chance I had a lot of fertility clients, so I thought about specializing in that, and at some point I thought the same thing about clients with digestive issues. Over time I realized that for me, seeing people with the exact same issue over and over was burning me out a little. I like variety. I still see clients for fertility issues, but it's not the bulk of my practice, and I think this balance works better for everyone concerned.

NLP and hypnosis teachers and practitioners Sarah and Shawn Carson told me about the importance of finding a niche:

"One of the quickest ways to building a practice is to choose a niche. Niche is important because it establishes you as the authority in your community. When people have your niche problem, they will automatically think of you. And of course you will still get lots of other clients too because when you are the expert in one area, people will believe you are also skilled in other areas."

Pamela Herrick, who, as I mentioned, lives in a small, rural community, thinks of niche differently: "For my practice, the key to success has been to specialize. I am the only full-time Thai massage therapist within a thirty-minute drive." Her niche is the kind of bodywork that she does. Similar to Pamela's experience, as my practice has evolved, I've begun to combine Reiki, reflexology, and hypnosis in the same session, and this is another way I define my niche, further differentiating me from other practitioners.

Is it better to offer more?

New practitioners often ask me if I see clients more for Reiki, hypnosis, or reflexology and if it's better to add more modalities to their practice.

I've seen practitioners who include a laundry list of techniques and modalities on their business card. Don't get me wrong: I think continuing education is vital, and I love taking new classes and learning new techniques and models of healing—but I'm not planning on adding more to my practice. I like variety, and I like having different tools I can use depending on the client and the issue that they're seeking to treat. But I also think it's really important to be thoroughly trained and knowledgeable about what you do, rather than diluting your practice with too many different things. If you're just starting out as a new practitioner, stick with one modality and become really proficient at it. Then, if you're truly interested in learning something else, study it for a while and see if you want to add it into your practice.

Sometimes people want to race through getting all these different modalities under their belt, or they love taking classes, but never get started with their practice as they keep waiting and focusing on accruing more knowledge. Remember that taking a weekend class in something doesn't make you an expert. It can also be confusing to your clients, because then they have to pick from among the laundry list of services you offer. Moreover, from a marketing perspective, it's easier to specialize in one modality—it's easier to explain, and it's more focused. It's a mouthful for me to say the three things I do, and that's definitely a drawback. Keep it simple as you get really good at what you do, and then expand from there if you feel called to do so.

Worries about competition

Sometimes new practitioners (and seasoned practitioners as well) worry about competition from others. The more you define your niche, the less competition you'll feel. When you're working with clients who are the perfect fit for your skills—your expertise, the things you're passionate and knowledgeable about, your life experiences—you'll do your best work. There's no way another practitioner can replicate your style, and people pick up on this authenticity, so that in the long run you'll attract the clients who need what you uniquely offer.

I like to remind myself that my ideal clients will find me if I stay true to myself, do my best, and continue with my personal practice (which for me is my meditation practice, taught within the system of Reiki).

Another Reiki practice opened very near Frans Stiene's office and school in Australia, but it didn't bother him. In fact, he thought it was a good thing:

"In essence, when we see someone as our competition, then this is based on our own insecurity. When we know as practitioners or teachers that we are doing the best that we can, 110 percent, then we have no fear of anybody teaching in our area, or neighborhood.

"This is also based on our own faith in what we do, faith within our practice and in what we teach. This faith is not established straight away; we need to work on this through our own personal practice [within the system of Reiki, or whatever meditation practice you have]. Through doing the meditations, we start to gain faith in the teachings and in what we do. This faith in turn gives us a solid foundation so that we do not see other practitioners or teachers as competitors."

Here's how Thai massage therapist and coach Pamela Herrick views competition living in a rural town:

"When I opened my private practice here in the Hudson Valley, a dear friend of mine and an experienced massage therapist said to me, 'Honey, sadly there is no end of pain in the world.' She helped me to see my practice and the community I work in as a glass half full.

"She told me to get treatment with every therapist in town, to see them as my colleagues, and to recognize that we are not in competition. The truth is, there is more need in any community than we could ever hope to meet."

Homework: Define your niche

+ What kinds of clients do you want to work with?
+ What interests and personal experiences do you have that might inform your niche?

7

Heart-Centered Marketing

Now that you've given some thought to the kinds of clients you want to work with, I'll focus on how to reach these clients through your marketing efforts. I'll give you a range of possibilities to explore, from in-person to online activities and everything in between.

What if you're not into marketing?

Before I started my practice, I thought I hated anything to do with marketing. I was surprised to realize as I went along that marketing is simply connecting in a focused way with people who need what you offer. And as Pamela Herrick's massage therapist friend pointed out: "Sadly, there is no end of pain in the world." People need what you're offering!

I think the concept of heart-centered marketing pairs naturally with the kind of work that wellness practitioners do. According to small-business expert Mark Silver, heart-centered marketing can help "create effective and profitable businesses whose actions and presence reflect the same love and caring in the work [you] love most."

Silver takes this thought even further, saying: "It's hard to believe, but you can find love in the daily actions of marketing, sales, systems, strategic planning, and other necessary business actions. [I've] found that every act of business can be an act of love, and in fact it's the only kind of world [I] want to live in."

This a somewhat radical idea, isn't?

Business expert Leonie Dawson agrees:

"If there's one big huge honkin' mistake I see new business owners making, it's that they aren't willing to tell people what they do and ask for the sale. The author Fabienne Fredrickson has a good analogy about this. She calls it 'Share Your Brownies!'

"Imagine you have a whole bunch of friends over to your house. And you decide to make brownies. So you head off into the kitchen, and you bake them. And as they are baking, your friends keep popping in and saying 'Oh my gosh! That smells so good! What are you doing in here? What are you making?' And you won't tell them. Because baking brownies is your gift, your offering to the world. But to talk about it would be too salesy. So you hide your brownies from your friends. And you eat them by yourself in the kitchen.

"The lesson here is: Don't hide your brownies!

"Have you told your friends/family/biz contacts/mama's group/ drum circle/knitting clatch what you do? And if not, why not?

"You've got to be willing to take control of your destiny, say what you do with pride, and ask for the sale. Not in a pushy, dirty, icky way, but in a genuine, 'I love you and I have a solution to your problem if you're called' kind of way."

Heart-centered marketing is the place I want to come from. When you're connecting with prospective clients, marketing from a heart-centered place, it's much less about selling to people. Rather, it's about connecting with people who need what you offer. It's about helping prospective clients feel comfortable with you, and better understand how what you do can help them, as you build trust along the way in moving toward the right time to work together.

As a practitioner, you're likely a people person, and that's part of the reason you're in this kind of work. But if this idea of heart-centered marketing doesn't resonate with you, then having your own practice might not be right for you. You might be better off working in a spa or a doctor's office or some other kind of setting where someone else is doing the marketing and getting the word out there, and you're just focusing on your work. Both approaches can be ripe with opportunity, but it's important to get clear about what will work best for you.

So assuming that you *are* interested in setting up your own practice, what are the first steps in spreading the word to potential clients?

Crafting your pitch

Like defining your niche market, crafting your pitch is also an ongoing process that begins with establishing a baseline description of your services that you'll revise, refine, and hone over time. It's taken me years to get good at describing what I do, which is why I'm here to help you get a jump start on the process.

The most important thing to remember in crafting your pitch is to describe what you do in a way that conveys how you can help somebody with their problem(s). In other words, you need to address the WIIFM—*What's in it for me?*

Often, practitioners try to simply describe the work that they do. To a prospective client this can sound like jargon, especially if you don't know a thing about reflexology or hypnosis, for example. When I used to tell people I offer Reiki, hypnosis, and reflexology, I would often watch their eyes glaze over as they wondered what any of those things are while nodding along—or they would just tune out entirely.

We're naturally hard-wired to think: "What's in it for me?" So always, always, put yourself in your potential client's shoes as you think about how to talk about what you do, describing it in their terms and from their perspective. For example, I might say something like, "I work with people navigating a major life transition—whether it's a career or relationship or health issue—using Reiki, hypnosis, and reflexology to help them find balance and connect to their intuition."

Describing your approach

Once you've addressed the WIIFM, the next step in crafting your pitch is to describe your approach. This is where you explain your philosophy of health, and how it relates to your discipline or wellness modality. In doing this, think about how you're distinct in what you do—your unique approach. Also, think about how you want to be perceived by your clients and the public.

I want to come across as grounded and professional, as well as positive and friendly. Maybe you want to come across as analytical and science-based in your approach by referencing research applicable to your discipline. Or maybe you want to come across as super creative and a little out there—helping others bow to the mysteries of the universe! Or maybe you want to be more formal and specialized, like the colleague I mentioned who works with new trial lawyers, to help them be more confident in the courtroom.

Once you know how you want to appear to clients, think carefully about the kind of tone that your target audience will respond to best. For example, lawyers are likely going to respond to a different kind of language than artists.

I'm reaching out to people who are open to integrative therapies, but may not have had a lot of diverse or direct experience with them. Maybe you want clients who are really familiar with, and big fans of, whatever wellness modality you use. Maybe you love the challenge of working with populations that aren't particularly open to the work that you do. Thinking about your niche and ideal clients is key to crafting your pitch, and will help you better describe who you are and phrase your approach in language that your ideal clients can best understand.

Particularly in the healing arts, it's really important to let your personality come through in your website, your newsletter, or whatever marketing vehicles you use so that prospective clients can get a sense of you, because the therapeutic relationship is so important. People want to go to a practitioner they trust and feel comfortable with, and the more you can convey who you are and what it's like to work with you before a new client meets you, the better. Done properly, you'll be attracting your ideal clients, which, of course, is your ultimate goal.

Homework: Building the foundation of a pitch

As you start out in practice, your pitch for your services can be as simple as a few sentences. To build the foundation of your pitch, ask yourself:

- How do you want to be perceived by your clients and the public?
- What do you want your tone to be?
- Take a few moments to fill in this sentence by business expert Alicia Dunhams: "My name is [your name] and I help [target audience] be/do/have [value you provide] so that [results].

Here's my example:

My name is Deborah Flanagan. I help new wellness practitioners build successful businesses, so they can reach more clients, maximize their income, and enjoy their work.

8

How To Find Clients in Person

Over the years, I've found that it's useful to have several different vehicles for finding new clients. This way you're not reliant just on one source that can dry up unexpectedly. For example, if the doctor who refers patients to you closes his practice, you'll still have other avenues for reaching new clients.

Because personal connection is so important in wellness therapies, seeking out face-to-face interaction can be a great way to meet potential clients. Here are some ways to engage with potential clients in person:

+ Free intros
+ Partnerships
+ Referrals

Free intros

A free intro can be used in many different ways, and can be a great way to introduce yourself to potential clients. You'll explain what you do and how it works, and possibly give a brief sample. Make sure you have some visuals to make your booth or space look inviting, and strive to look professional in the way that you dress and in your materials.

You can get creative in thinking up possible venues in which to meet potential clients. For example, here are some of the free intros I've participated in:

- I offered a brief talk and a sample mini Reiki session at my local gym. I'd become friendly with one of the class instructors, and I did a free intro a few times at her boot camp classes. (Note: offer Reiki sample sessions either before or at least an hour or two after class. With such an intense and extreme sympathetic nervous system workout, the parasympathetic, balancing effects of Reiki will be harder to notice and experience immediately after.)
- I participated in a few health fairs for corporations wanting to offer their employees ways to reduce stress and enhance wellness. The wellness fairs had thirty to forty booths set up for various practitioners to offer free samples, hand out brochures and informational materials, and answer questions.
- I did sample mini sessions at the neurologist's office I previously mentioned.
- I participated in an open house at the New York Open Center (a holistic education center where I did some of my training). They offered mini-sessions, and I was paid a small fee to offer 15-minute Reiki sessions.

Other places to consider giving a free intro: service organizations, colleges, churches, libraries, and book stores. You might also consider joining a small business group for additional support (which might be another place you could give a free intro!).

The four most important things you should do at a free intro:

- Have your appointment book handy in case people want to book an appointment. As an incentive, you can also offer a discount if they book a future appointment that day.

- Hand out your business card and any other relevant information, such as your brochure.
- Capture potential clients' email addresses, so you can stay in touch and send your e-newsletter to them. Have a clipboard with a sign-up sheet.
- Email everyone who signs up for the e-newsletter as soon as you can (within a week, if not the day after the event). In the email, tell them what kind of information they can expect from your newsletter, how often you send it, etc. You can also offer a discount if they book an appointment by a certain deadline.

Astrology coach and spiritual counselor Maria Rodriguez agrees: "I think the most important thing is to make absolutely sure that you collect email addresses. Because then you can keep people in the loop, letting them know what you're doing next and what might interest them. For example, in the spring you can send clients an email saying 'it's a great time for spring cleaning, come in for a session,' or in January you can write about how you can help support them with their new year's resolutions."

Maria is great at free intros, but it turns out I'm much more comfortable online than off. I just didn't get that many clients through these kinds of activities, and to be honest, I don't really enjoy doing them (and yes, I think those two things are related!).

This is another piece of heart-centered marketing: if you really don't enjoy writing an e-newsletter and emailing it to your clients, but you love face-to-face meetings, find what resonates with you instead of forcing yourself to do things you dislike. That being said, I do encourage you to try a variety of marketing strategies (and try them more than once). Don't just assume you don't like something—this cuts you off from the possibility of discovering something new.

There's a difference between truly going outside your comfort zone and feeling initial discomfort but then growing more comfortable and building a new skill. So find a balance. You won't know until you do it. There are always certain tasks in your business that you're going to enjoy doing less than others—but that doesn't mean you can neglect them. For example, while I don't love giving free intros, I tried out a lot of different ways to offer them, and this helped me figure out what works for me. Experimentation is the name of the game, as you see what marketing strategies generate the biggest payoff and benefits while still being in alignment with what you enjoy doing.

Partners

Creating partnerships is another way to build your client base. For example, I partner with a nutritionist who used to have an office in the same office suite as me. The nutritionist had previously sent her patients to another practitioner for hypnosis to help with weight loss and emotional eating. The hypnotist relocated to Connecticut, and since the nutritionist didn't know another hypnotist to recommend, she was still sending her clients in New York City to this woman in Connecticut! Now we both refer clients to each other as appropriate.

I also reached out to a pediatric gastroenterologist as a result of my relationship with the nutritionist. The nutritionist had attended a lecture where this doctor gave a talk about stress and its negative effects on digestive issues in children. During her residency in Boston, she'd seen the positive effects of hypnosis on her patients, but didn't know of anyone in New York who used hypnosis with children.

I followed up with the pediatric doctor, making clear that while my focus wasn't primarily on treating children, I was interested in working with them more, and that I had had positive results working with adults with severe digestive issues.

Here are some other examples of people you could potentially partner with:

+ A neurologist, if your ideal clients experience chronic headaches
+ A pain specialist, if your ideal clients deal with chronic pain

+ A dentist, if your ideal clients have a dental phobia
+ A physical therapy office, if your ideal clients have specific kinds of injuries

Remember to be patient, as it takes time to develop a partnership— first you must demonstrate your professionalism and credibility, and develop trust with the other practitioner. I also like to offer the potential partner a sample session, so that they can experience the benefits of my work. And if I'm going to refer clients back to these partners, I like to experience or find out more about their work as well, so I'm able to recommend them without reservation.

Referrals

In every business, referrals are a key way to find new clients. People are highly responsive to their friends' recommendations, because they trust their judgment. Especially with wellness work, because it's so intimate, clients feel vulnerable and want to find a practitioner they can trust to hold a space of healing for them as they share their issues and challenges. Let your clients know you're building your practice, and that you would love it if they could let people who might benefit from or be interested in your practice (friends, coworkers, and family members) know about your services.

I know some practitioners, such as Maria Rodriguez, who've built their whole practice on referrals:

"I do meet-up groups for astrology, and participants often schedule private readings with me. At the end of the reading, these clients often say: 'Do you mind if I refer you to one of my friends?' Or, 'I referred you to one of my friends; is that okay?'"

I'm sure you can anticipate her answer: "Of course!"

Maria talks about the pros and cons of relying almost entirely on referrals: "There's an ebb and flow getting clients this way, but it works well for me because I also teach. I think once somebody likes you and spreads the word, it really does make a huge difference. I'm also getting some interesting clients who I would never expect to want astrology. I'm not even getting the glassy-eyed stares anymore—the clients I see are very open to it."

More ways to get referrals

When I first started my practice, I sent an email to friends letting them know about my new business. I offered a friends/family discount, and also asked them to let people know who might be interested in my practice. I was surprised to find that the friends I least expected to be interested in a session were the ones who ended up booking appointments. This goes to show you never know who will be interested in what you offer.

You can also reach out to other people you come into contact with regularly. For example, my beautiful Brazilian hairstylist, Ana, asked for a few business cards when I told her about my practice. People tell their hairstylists their problems and issues, so this can be a great resource. Think about people in your life who might come into contact with the kinds of clients you're looking for.

Occasionally, I've asked clients at the end of my e-newsletter to forward it to someone who might benefit from my services. You could also do this in person after your client's session, but that hasn't felt right for me, so I haven't done it.

Homework: Finding potential clients for your practice

Think about the needs of your ideal clients/niche market and other places where these potential clients are getting those needs met.

- Brainstorm three places where you can offer a free intro.
- List three potential partners and how you can approach them.
- Write down three ideas you can use to get referrals.

9

How to Find Clients Online

The Internet can be an amazing tool for reaching out to niche communities. There are numerous ways to engage with potential clients online, including:

+ Your website
+ E-newsletter/blog
+ Social media
+ Guest posts on other blogs/websites

Bear in mind that you don't have to use all these strategies—some are more crucial to every business than others, and as with in-person marketing strategies, you'll likely have more success sticking to techniques that are comfortable for you. But I think it is important to briefly discuss more advanced marketing strategies, to give you a sense of where you can go once you create a strong foundation for your business.

Your website

It doesn't need to be complicated or elaborate, but I do think it's important to have your own website. It could be just a couple of simple pages containing your bio and contact information, and information about your approach and the modality you practice. A website will enable prospective clients to read more about you and the work that you do, whether people come into contact with you in person, through a friend or one of your partners, or by searching online for the services you offer.

I was lucky to have a good friend with a small design firm, and she guided me through the process of creating my website. A lot has changed since I created my site, and now it's much easier. There are web design companies that offer a basic template, and it's much less expensive than it used to be.

Even if it's basic, you want your website to look professional and give a sense of who you are—if you think about it, encountering your website may be the first time a prospective client meets you. It's just like your mom used to say: first impressions count!

Your website should include:

+ Your office address and phone number (on every page, so clients can easily contact you without having to hunt for your contact information)
+ A way to sign up for your e-newsletter
+ A professional-looking photo of you
+ A brief bio, including your qualifications and training/certifications/licenses
+ Your approach and description of what you do (which I covered in Chapter 7)
+ Information about your sessions
  + Rates (if you feel comfortable posting this info online)
  + Session length options
  + Days/times you're available to see clients
+ Answers to frequently asked questions
+ Your blog if you have one, or want to start one

While having a website is important, just having one won't automatically bring you clients, as hypnosis and NLP teacher and practitioner Sarah Carson found:

"There are a number of things that I was naively unaware of when first setting out. I remember working really hard to get our website up and running, and I truly thought that once it was launched my phone would be ringing off the hook . . . well, that didn't exactly happen!

"My husband Shawn asked me how I had gotten clients in my previous job, which was rather funny because as a kindergarten teacher my "clients" were 5 years old, and they just showed up in my classroom on the first day of school. I had never had to go out and find clients before, and hadn't really considered anything further than hanging out my shingle on the World Wide Web.

"As I consider the job now, there is so very much more to running a micro business than simply seeing clients. We need to be astute marketers, be able to write good copy, be the head accountant, understand and keep up with current trends in social marketing, have the ability to keep our website up to date, have an understanding of SEO (search engine optimization), or have the external support to do these things. I think that it's useful to have these things in mind when starting out, and be ready to jump in and learn as these things change so quickly!"

Again, getting your website up and running is a key tool for providing prospective clients with more information about you, whether they meet you online or offline. It's also an indicator to prospective clients that you are a committed professional—you're invested enough in the success of your business to have a website—and it also helps build trust as they get to know you.

E-newsletter/blog

I have a background as a writer, so creating an e-newsletter (which I later turned into a blog) was a natural marketing choice for me. Even if you don't like writing, a newsletter is a great way to keep in touch with your clients, and it doesn't have to be wordy or involve a lot of writing.

Figure out a frequency that works for you—quarterly, monthly, twice a month, or weekly. I send my e-newsletter out twice a month and would like to increase its frequency to weekly. You'll need to experiment to get a feel for how often you have news to share and how often clients want to hear from you—try a frequency that feels right and see how your clients respond.

An e-newsletter is a great reminder to your clients to book an appointment, as well as a tool to educate them on the benefits of the work that you do and how it can help them (remember WIIFM—*What's in it for me?*). Often when I send my e-newsletter out, clients contact me that day or a few days later to book an appointment.

A couple of years ago, I started posting my e-newsletter content as a blog on my website. It helps your SEO (search-engine optimization), which just means you'll be more likely to show up higher in a list of Google or other search engine results. It also offers visitors to your website more information and resources if they aren't signed up for your e-newsletter.

Remember to always offer prospective clients a way to sign up for your e-newsletter whenever you do in-person events.

What to include in your e-newsletter:

- Articles about the benefits of what you do or other topics of interest
- Updates on studies showing the efficacy of your modality
- Answers to frequently asked questions you hear from your clients
- Self-help tips your clients can try at home to prolong the effects of their sessions with you

- Special promotions/discounts
- Gift certificate reminders for holiday gifts
- If you teach, information about upcoming classes or workshops

Just like with your website, business cards, and other marketing materials, write your e-newsletter in a tone that conveys how you want to be perceived, so that current and potential clients can develop trust in you and your skills and get a sense of who you are.

Social media

As a new practitioner, I think you should devote only a small portion of marketing time to building a social media presence. It's worth doing, as another way to market your services and expand your reach, but it shouldn't be a top priority. You have much less control of your content on social media and are subject to any changes the social media provider makes (for example, Facebook has made several changes over the past few years limiting how often fans see content you post on your Facebook business page). If you're already using certain kinds of social media, start with what you're already doing (e.g. if you're already using Facebook, Twitter, Instagram, Pinterest, or LinkedIn, start with whichever one(s) you already use and enjoy).

Facebook

For example, I have a Facebook page for my business. I keep it separate from my personal profile, because I want to keep that boundary between my personal and professional lives. You'll need to figure out what feels comfortable for you. I enjoy posting things on my Facebook page. It's a way to stay connected with current clients, but in my experience, it hasn't been a way for me to get new clients.

I do post my newsletter and occasional things about my practice on my personal page, as well as my business page. My friends sometimes become clients, or refer somebody to me because of what I post on Facebook, so it can be a more informal way to let your friends know about your practice. And I'm doing it in the context of my e-newsletter/ blog posts, writing about things that may interest them whether they come for a session or not, such as ways to de-stress or sleep better. I make sure to only post things related to my business on my personal page occasionally, so that I'm not bombarding my friends with information about my practice.

Twitter, LinkedIn, Google+ and Pinterest

I don't enjoy using these networks as much, so I don't spend a lot of time on them other than posting my e-newsletter. Again, especially when you're just starting out, social media should not be your main focus. You can ease into integrating social media into your business once you're further along.

Guest posts on other blogs/websites

In addition to my e-newsletter and blog, I enjoy writing guest posts for health and wellness-related websites such as MindBodyGreen.com and YourTango.com. If you go to these sites, many of them have writers' guidelines you can look at to figure out the best way to approach them and pitch an article. Most such posts aren't paid, but writing guest posts can help you in several ways:

- Directing traffic to your website
- Establishing you as an expert in your field
- Reaching new clients
- Improving your website's SEO

I haven't had a ton of new clients come to me through writing guest posts, but if you like writing (yes, I was an English major!) it can be a way to expand your reach. Again, this shouldn't be a top priority when you're just starting out, but it's something to consider once you get the more important marketing pieces mentioned above in place.

Don't be afraid to try out new tools

I can't say this enough: experiment! And then experiment some more! There are so many ways to reach the prospective clients who are looking for help and need what you offer. Get creative, and know that not everything you do will necessarily work, but there's a learning curve, and you're in the process of figuring out what *does* work. And keep track of how your clients find you, so you know what strategies are most effective. I highly recommend that you include a question on your client intake form about this to help you keep track.

Homework: Developing your online marketing strategy

+ If you don't already have a website, what's the next smallest step you need to take to create one? If you do have a website, is there content you need to add to it from the suggestions mentioned above?
+ What is the right frequency for sending your e-newsletter?
+ What are three topics you can write about in your e-newsletter?
+ Is there a social media platform you're already using (and enjoy) where you can start to incorporate information about your practice?

10

Reaching Your Niche Market

Now that I've given you ideas for reaching prospective clients both in-person and online, I want you to get more specific with your marketing. Take a moment to review the various marketing vehicles for finding new clients described in the previous two chapters.

Once you've done that, I want you to get in the mind of your ideal client and niche market, and think about places your ideal client frequents, the kinds of things they purchase, what they read, etc. If you have one or two clients who you especially like and feel connected with, you can have them in mind as you think about these details.

- Where do your ideal clients shop—do they go to health food stores or Whole Foods, for example? Certain bookstores? Cafes, juice bars, coffee shops?
- What magazines, websites, or newspapers do they read?
- What hobbies do they have?
- What kind of physical activity do they do? For example, do they like yoga? Do they go to the gym?
- What are their other distinguishing characteristics? Are they new moms? Do they have a certain health condition?

In addition to using your imagination to get into their mind-set, you can talk to your clients and ask them questions. People usually like to be helpful. If you say, "You're my ideal client, would you mind if I asked you a few questions to help me find more clients like you?"—well, who wouldn't like to hear that?

As I've said, I found online marketing to be a surprisingly effective way to reach my ideal clients. I didn't think my website would help me find clients as much as it did. But it may be different for you. For instance, I live in New York City, but Thai massage therapist and coach Pamela Herrick lives in a small town in the Hudson Valley, and she posts business cards and flyers around town. That's the way I found her—I saw her card at the local health food store. She's found her approach to online marketing has changed as her practice has evolved:

"When I began in 2002, a well-designed rack card in places where my ideal client hangs out worked to keep a steady stream of new clients. I also asked clients for referrals, letting them know that I was building a practice. I offered occasional classes of interest to my clients, and did snail mailings about twice a year.

"Today, my marketing efforts are entirely different. I still leave business cards around town, but new clients increasingly come to me from my website and blog, even personal referrals are a smaller part of my practice growth. I continue to offer classes and workshops as practice builders, and I email my client list with event updates and links to blog posts about self-care about every six weeks.

"I don't encourage Yelp as a marketing tool. In a small community it is not used (I can tell you the name of practically every business owner in town!). Also, because I am not available for immediate massage services, web listings are a poor fit for my therapeutic practice."

Once you've thought about the places your prospective clients frequent, online or offline, you can post information about your practice in those places. For offline spaces, you can figure out how to be present in those places by offering a free intro or sample mini-sessions, etc., or posting your business card or flyer.

Remember that marketing is an ongoing process; there are always more ways to find the kinds of clients you want to work with, both online and in person, and your strategies for reaching them will evolve and change as you and your practice grow.

Homework: Reaching your niche market

+ List three places offline where you can pursue new business in person or post information about your practice.
+ List three places online where you can post information about your practice.

11

Packages, Promotions, & Publicity

In addition to thinking about *where* you can promote your practice online and offline, you'll want to figure out *how*—the specific terms you can offer. Packages and promotions can be another way to market your practice. Packages can offer ways to build ongoing relationships with your clients, and allow for a deeper treatment experience with the possibility of more comprehensive results. Promotions are great for encouraging new clients to give an unfamiliar treatment modality a try.

Creating a package of services

Offering discounted session packages can be a great way to encourage clients to return and commit to a treatment plan. In many ways it can be easier than treatment session-by-session: clients save money, they don't have to think about whether they should book another session, and you're able to offer them continuity in their treatment.

To start, think about how many sessions it might take to create noticeable change in a certain issue area for your clients. For a hypnotist, offering a three-session quit-smoking package, or a ten-session fertility package, might be a great way to help your clients achieve the results they want. Similarly, for Reiki, reflexology, or massage, offering a three-session intro package can be a good way to help clients measure the results and benefits of treatment, since one session often isn't enough when dealing with certain health conditions or other issues.

You'll also need to calculate how much of a discount you can afford to give. For a package, you probably don't want to discount your services as deeply as you might in offering a single-session promotion. I think 10 to 15 percent is a good general range. The more sessions they purchase, the bigger the discount. For example, I offered a three-session package, which was approximately an 8 percent savings, and a ten-session package, which was approximately a 12 percent savings.

I offered packages until a year or so ago. Among my clients—and again, your client base may be different—it appealed to a handful of people, but it wasn't a driving factor in whether clients came back and booked another session. I was surprised by this, because I had thought it would make a bigger difference. I also had to keep track of when packages expired, and how many sessions clients had left in their packages, and it ended up taking more administrative time than I expected. Since so few of my clients were using packages, I stopped offering them. But creating packages might be something you want to experiment with to see if your clients are responsive to them.

Creating promotional discounts

I've also offered a range of promotions over the years, especially when I was first starting out.

Here are some ideas for you to play with:

- $10 (or another amount) off the first session for new clients.
- During a holiday or specific time of year, a certain dollar discount.
- A discount for clients toward their next session if they buy a gift certificate during the holidays for someone else.

I used to offer $15 off a session during clients' birthday months. Not many clients took advantage of it, but it was a good reminder of my practice and services, and people liked that I was wishing them a happy birthday, and I liked being able to send a personalized email as well. My online booking system had a tool to set this up and automatically sent clients an email on their birthday.

I also experimented with deal-of-the-day promotions like Groupon. I recommend approaching this strategy with caution—if you want experience seeing a lot of new clients to hone your skills, it's not a bad idea, but you're not going to make much money from it. It also wasn't a way to build a relationship and get returning clients. In a scenario like this, you're offering such a heavily discounted deal that to then convert clients to paying full price is a really big jump. These promotions attract clients who value a cheap deal above all.

This same principle is something to consider whenever you offer a discount. Be clear on your goals and the type of client you want to attract. At one point I told clients if they referred somebody to me and that person came for a session, the referrer would get 50 percent off a session—but no one took me up on it. Again, discounts didn't seem to appeal to the majority of my clients. On the other hand, I got this idea from a very successful massage therapist and it worked well for him, so again, you'll have to be willing to try out different strategies.

Offering these various packages and promotions helped me realize that I don't like offering a lot of discounts—I want people to come for a session because they see the value of it, and think it's worth paying my full rate. And if they don't, that's absolutely fine—they aren't my ideal client, and there are practitioners out there who might be perfect for what they're looking for. As I was building my practice many of these packages and promotions were helpful, and then as my practice evolved my feelings about them changed.

Gift certificates

I've offered gift certificates since I began my practice. I think it's a good idea to offer them—they don't require me to offer my services for less than I feel they're necessarily worth, as discounts do—but I have some reservations. Over the years, I've found that often the recipients of the certificates don't become regular clients. Although the purchaser of the gift certificate might love what I do—maybe they're a huge fan of Reiki or reflexology or hypnosis—the recipient sometimes isn't as interested, or doesn't consider those kinds of services a priority in their personal budgets.

That said, there are definitely exceptions to the rule: one new client told her husband she wanted a reflexology session for Christmas. He bought her a gift certificate and she was thrilled. Another client received a gift certificate from her friends for her birthday, because they knew she was really interested in Reiki.

Some things to consider when offering gift certificates:

+ Hard copy vs. email version: I offer both, but often people like the email version because then it can be a last minute gift idea that they can send to the recipient right away.
+ Expiration date: When does the gift certificate expire? Make sure you make this clear on the certificate, on your website, etc. Mine expire a year from purchase.
+ Transferability: Clients will ask you if they can use the certificate if the recipient doesn't use it. For my practice, gift certificates are nontransferable. It keeps it simple and is easier to keep track.
+ Payment options: How do you want people to pay for the gift certificate? Clients can use PayPal if they purchase a gift certificate on my website. Occasionally they mail me a check.

Remember, gift certificates are another administrative task that requires tracking and takes some time. I'll include the tracking spreadsheet for gift certificates that I use in Excel in the Business Starter Kit on my website (www.centertruehealth.com/business-starter-kit).

Getting publicity

While actively seeking publicity won't be an important part of building a practice for most wellness practitioners, and it wasn't for me either, I do want to address it briefly.

Four years into my practice, I had the good fortune to be featured in a segment on reflexology on *The Dr. Oz Show*, and I was also profiled in *O Magazine*. I've had many practitioners ask me about these experiences, so I'll share some details with you.

The producer for *The Dr. Oz Show* found my website and gave me a call. Things moved quickly. We talked about what the segment would be about (five self-help reflexology techniques viewers could use at home to help them with common ailments), and then we taped the show less than a week later.

The *O Magazine* article came about because one of my former co-workers is a freelance writer and had pitched an article about me a year before for a section in the magazine about career transitions and life changes. She never heard anything back about it. And then out of the blue, a year later, the editor she had pitched the article to came back to her and asked her to write the piece in three days! The magazine set up a photo shoot with me the following week.

If you're going to do media, it's all the more important to hone your pitch, as discussed in Chapter 7. You will want to think about what you know about the specific angle on the topic that a media outlet is taking, and how you can make bridges from those ideas back to your own core philosophy about the way you practice. A show segment or article isn't an opportunity to stand on a chair and say, "Call me at 555-5555 to book an appointment!" It is a chance to make clear to the audience that you know what you're talking about, and that you have a specific reason for approaching your work in the way that you do.

Both of my national media experiences were somewhat surreal, but also enjoyable. I was grateful for the opportunity to share the potential benefits of Reiki and reflexology (I hadn't incorporated hypnosis into my practice at that point), as well as the opportunity to be profiled. Did it help me get clients? Yes and no. I got a few new clients from the *Dr. Oz* segment, and I got a lot of email subscribers from it. I also had the opportunity to write an article about reflexology for the Dr. Oz website. Many more clients came to me through the piece in *O Magazine*, and I still see a few of those clients and Reiki students on a regular basis, which is absolutely wonderful.

The clients that came through *The Dr. Oz Show* were not my ideal clients, but the Oprah clients were, on the whole, fantastic. The article in *O Magazine* was specifically about transitions, and this spoke to exactly the kind of person I wanted to reach. The clients who came to me fell into a wide range of ages and races and income brackets and careers, but they were all my ideal kind of client: in the middle of a transition, and ready to make positive changes in their lives. They were fantastic to work with, and I could see firsthand the magic of Oprah's appeal to so many different kinds of women. It was really wonderful to witness. I've gone on to do other media appearances on TV, in print, and online. While these have been amazing opportunities, they aren't a direct way to bring in lots of clients—the time it takes to actively convince a media outlet to cover you, instead of having an opportunity fall into your lap, can be significant, and you never know how big of a payoff to expect. Indirectly, media coverage does help you find potential clients, because it can enhance your credibility and help establish you as an authority or expert in your field. If an opportunity comes your way, absolutely go for it, but I wouldn't recommend spending a lot of time trying to get publicity.

Homework: Creating packages, promotions, and gift certificates

+ Given the kind of work that you do, what kind of packages might work well with your treatment plans?
+ Write down three possible promotions you could offer.
+ Do you want to offer gift certificates? If so, do you want to offer print or emailable certificates, or both?

12

Building a Strong Client Base

Now that you have some ideas about how to pitch your services, who your ideal client is, and how to reach out to these clients with various in-person and online marketing vehicles, let's focus on the most important part of your practice—keeping your existing clients.

Having a successful practice full of happy clients is probably your number-one goal, right? I'll give you tips on how to how to nurture and build strong, healthy relationships with your clients, as well as how to handle challenging situations that might arise in a way that best supports you and allows you to take care of your own needs as a practitioner.

How to get clients to become regulars

One key to getting your clients to become regulars is to remember that the session extends beyond what happens when they're actually on the massage table or in the hypnosis chair. Establishing rapport when the client is booking an appointment, as well as at the beginning and end of the session, and following up after the session—all these things are really important as you build a relationship with each client.

I want my clients to feel as comfortable as possible, especially because they're often coming to me with a sensitive issue, and speaking from a place of vulnerability when they tell me about their problems. If clients feel supported—if they know that you're truly listening to them, that they can trust you, and that you're here to help them—all this will encourage them to come back.

In addition to making clients comfortable before, during, and after the session, come up with ways to stay in touch with them in between sessions. As I mentioned above, sending an e-newsletter regularly is a good reminder for clients to book a session if they need one. I always include a call to action (an instruction that provokes an immediate response) in the e-newsletter, prompting them to engage with my practice in an ongoing way. For example, "Feeling stressed? Contact me to schedule your next session."

Again, offering clients tips or articles about the work that you do, answers to frequently asked questions, and ways to be proactive in their health and wellbeing are some content suggestions to include in your newsletter that will help you build a relationship with them beyond the work you do in your office.

Pamela Herrick talks about how she works with her clients over time:

"Having a treatment plan and educating clients about the role of preventative care is key to building a practice. Many of my clients come at first to resolve a problem and remain for years. Once their initial complaint is successfully treated, I generally recommend a monthly Thai massage to prevent a recurrence and get all those amazing benefits from regular bodywork.

"For my clients with whom I have worked with over many years, our therapeutic relationship takes on a different tone with time. My role as witness to their changing health becomes increasingly valuable. I see subtle changes and can bring them to a client's conscious awareness, where they can work on them.

"Do I want clients to stay with me 'forever'? Not unless they want to. When your work together is complete, it is important to give clients permission to move on and to help them find other therapies as needed. I regularly refer to acupuncturists and other massage therapists when the time to leave arrives."

Creating a treatment plan

Clients often need to feel the support and guidance of some kind of treatment plan. I think some wellness practitioners learn a lot about developing a treatment plan during their training. I didn't learn much about this in my Reiki, hypnosis, or reflexology training, so I figured it out as I went.

Generally, I say three sessions in quick succession—once a week, for example—is a great way to evaluate if the work we're doing together is going to help or not, and then we take it from there with a personalized plan based on the client's needs. As I've worked in my practice, I realized that during the first session my intuition gives me some idea of how to work with this particular client. During the first session with a new client, see what comes up and moves, what they notice, how they respond consciously and unconsciously, and let this information guide your recommendations about treatment. This is a skill you'll develop over time, and you can incorporate the wisdom of your intuition into what you were taught in your training.

I think it's important to personalize the treatment plan. For example, I could see five clients for fertility issues, and to one of them I might say, "I think you need to come every week." To another I might say, "Come every couple of weeks," or "Come once a month," or "Come until you start noticing a change in your cycle or how you're feeling surrounding this issue." My recommendation takes into consideration the information they've given me in their intake form, other therapies they may be participating in, and my intuition about what they need. I also believe strongly in giving clients self-help techniques or homework they can do to extend and prolong the effects of their sessions. I like giving clients empowering tools to help themselves.

Astrology coach and spiritual counselor Maria Rodriguez puts it this way:

"I think the mark of a good practitioner is that you don't pigeon-hole. Like you said, you could have five people basically with the same problem, but you need to really concentrate on each person individually, and that's a testament to you as a practitioner that really wants people to see results and feel better. Just because a teacher told you what a treatment plan should be, or you read a treatment plan in a book, it doesn't necessarily mean it's right for every client."

Pamela Herrick agrees:

"My first Thai massage treatment for a new client includes developing a treatment plan together. Here's why:

"A treatment plan begins with a goal. Whether your sweet client's goal is relaxation or rotator cuff surgery recovery, you can build for them a plan to meet it. Clients want to know that you understand their problem, that you have successfully treated it before, and that you can give an approximation of how long it will take to resolve. When you have enough training and experience to do all three, your clients will trust that they are spending their healthcare budget (which is often limited) wisely with you.

"A treatment plan outlines what each of us will be responsible for to move the client to their goal. My job is to provide care, outline a time frame, monitor progress and advise self-care. My client's job is to (ahem!) *do* the self-care, observe for changes, and report them back to me.

"One of the loveliest goals I have ever had the privilege to work on for a client was this:

"My client, a mother of three girls in her late fifties, arrived with shoulder pain and restricted range of motion. When I asked her goal, she told me that she had lost her daughter to cancer several years before. She had promised her daughter that every year in winter she would lie down on her grave and make a snow angel for her. Winter was approaching, and my client knew that year it would be tricky, and no way was she going to break her promise to her dear girl.

"Together, we did it. She committed to a treatment schedule, I did my work, she did her homework. That winter, she made her snow angel and kept her promise.

"She has been my client ever since, and it is a relationship I cherish."

This is a beautiful and moving example of developing a relationship with a client, and helping them move forward with a very specific treatment plan.

Here are some additional practitioner responses to developing a treatment plan.

Frans Stiene had this to say:

"It completely depends on the client—sometimes I give clients a mediation to practice. Or maybe I give them a precept to think about. But not every client is open to this, as many clients want you to heal them and they aren't ready to take responsibility. Therefore we need to come to the level of our clients and act, teach, and treat them according to what they need and are ready for. Sometimes we can say come for three treatments, or we can say come for twenty, but again it depends on the client if they want this or not.

"But I do agree it's good to make a kind of plan, a plan which suits the individual needs of your client."

Polarity teacher and practitioner Gary Strauss offers a big-picture view of treatment, and discusses the importance of keeping client notes to chart each client's progress:

"I do think having a sense of treatment over time is important, while balancing this with being in the moment to focus on the task at hand. It's a duality to be real and open to the moment, and then to also have a sense of being able to hold the client's treatment over time.

"Be present and have an ability to manage your relation to their healing and unfolding life journey. This takes time to acquire, and this is why I encourage my students to keep case studies/client session documentations in the beginning. These will help you hold and track the client's process and journey."

Alternately, Reiki teacher and practitioner Joanna Crespo prefers to keep sessions more open-ended:

"I don't create a treatment plan. I leave it up to my clients to decide. As a matter of fact, I usually ask them to wait for a week before making another appointment with me."

Similarly, hypnosis and NLP trainers and practitioners Sarah and Shawn Carson keep their work with clients flexible, recognizing the difficulty in predicting how quickly clients will change:

"We don't have a 'treatment plan' in the traditional sense. Depending upon the client's issue, we'll suggest the possible number of sessions we may need, and ask them to commit to these.

"Working with hypnosis for fertility is twelve sessions, and we do have a little more structure in the first two sessions as we explore the potential 'blockages' that may be inhibiting conception. This gives us some idea of a roadmap for future sessions.

"Our Quit Smoking protocol is three sessions. We truly believe that 'All we are is changing,' and what we may have laid out in a plan in week one will certainly have changed by the time we get to see them the following week. Having flexibility is key."

This variety of approaches gives you a broad range of options as you explore and create your own treatment protocols to use with your clients. All the practitioners interviewed above agree on one thing: each client is different and his or her needs in receiving treatment will be different as well. Being flexible is the name of the game with this kind of work.

The life cycle of your client base

In my experience, client relationships fall into three categories:

+ As needed: As-needed clients are probably the most prevalent in my practice. They come for a single session when they feel like they really need it, and are usually dealing with some kind of physical or emotional crisis.

+ Periodic in-depth: These clients come when they're having an issue, whether it be chronic or acute, and they come until it gets better, which might take between three and ten sessions. They sometimes return at a later date if another issue comes up and they need additional help and support.

+ Perennials: Perennials are clients that I've been seeing for years. Most of them come once a month for maintenance, in an effort to be proactive in taking care of themselves and their health.

Because my focus is helping clients in the midst of a major transition, it makes sense that I would see more clients who fall into categories 1 and 2. This mix will vary from practitioner to practitioner, depending on the focus of their practice.

Personally, I like variety, and I like that clients move on once their issue is resolved. Of course, I also like seeing clients if they come back, which offers the opportunity for a deeper practitioner/client relationship. And as my practice changes, the clients change. So I probably wouldn't want to still be working with the clients I had when I first started out, because I've grown as a practitioner, and the kinds of people and issues I attract have changed as a result. You'll notice this, too, as your own practice evolves and changes.

The life cycle of your client relationships will also vary depending on the kind of practitioner you are. For example, my hypnosis clients usually are coming for a very specific issue, and it's easy to measure if they've overcome their phobia or not. My fertility clients will come either until they get pregnant or throughout their pregnancy, and then once their baby is born they stop coming for sessions, or they don't come as often.

Astrology coach and spiritual counselor Maria Rodriquez usually hears from clients once or twice a year because of the nature of her work—she's giving her clients a reading about the upcoming six months or a year, so her cycle is not as consistent as that of someone who offers reflexology, for example.

Now you have some ideas on how to build positive relationships with your clients, personalizing a treatment plan based on each client's needs coupled with your own professional philosophy and preferences. Next, we'll address how to handle various client challenges that might arise.

13

Client Challenges

Many of the challenges you might face when dealing with clients have to do with boundaries. From how to establish your cancellation policy, to what to do when a client shows up late, to how to gracefully fire a client if it's not a good fit, I'll give you some ideas to help you figure out your boundaries in relation to a range of client challenges.

Creating healthy boundaries

I think Gary Strauss best sums up how to develop healthy boundaries as a practitioner, and how these boundaries will evolve over time:

"It takes time to understand boundaries and relations with clients, and then it changes as you mature. In the beginning my boundaries were much more strict. I think that was good, because it made up for what I lacked in experience. It's better to have stronger boundaries when you're a new practitioner, and looking at the formal Practice Standards and Code of Ethics prescribed by your discipline (polarity, reflexology, etc.) is a good place to start.

"Your clients are clients first and foremost (vs. your friends), and it's true our relationships with our clients deepen over time. This work is so intimate, and we have a responsibility to hold the space for each client's unfolding with their health and wellbeing.

"This is the idea I like to hold in my mind with each client I see: 'I love you, and it's your life, and our work together is not about me.'"

I think it's so important to constantly remind yourself that this work isn't about you—to make sure your ego doesn't get in the way of guiding and helping your clients do what they need to do to heal, move forward, etc. Reiki teacher and practitioner Joanna Crespo agrees, and puts it this way:

"You don't want to go home with your clients, and you don't want to grow old with your clients."

This is an important boundary to be aware of. Gary Strauss articulates it this way: "As the practitioner, you want to be everything and nothing to your client."

In other words, you want to create a neutral relationship with your clients, giving them as much as you can while being mindful that you are a facilitator, not your client's friend, and that they will move on if and when they're ready.

As practitioners, we truly want our clients to get well and/or achieve their goals. It may take one session, it may take ten, but I think that both the client and the practitioner intuitively know when the relationship is working or not.

Additionally, integrative hypnosis practitioner and trainer Melissa Tiers points out that dealing with challenging clients can be extremely beneficial:

"Some of my most powerful learning has come from the clients that I didn't help as I would have liked. They inspired me to keep trying new approaches, expanding my tool kit, and sometimes changing my whole view of certain conditions. I think these sessions taught me how to dance in ways I never knew I could."

I think it's also important to be able to picture each client with all their resources, completely healthy and whole. I always tell my students, if you can't picture your client as healthy in your mind's eye, you shouldn't see them. Don't be limited by the disease, or the limitations they're coming to you with. You want to be able to hold the space for their healing to occur.

Again, Gary Strauss puts it this way:

"At the end of the session, imagine all the systems in your client's body working, breathing, resonating, finding their way, moving through her body and her life, cementing the work that you just did together."

How to deal with clients who are late

I'm often asked by new practitioners how to deal with clients who are late to their appointments. Since I see clients back-to-back, I simply explain that we'll fit as much as we can into the session, but that the session needs to end on time to be fair to my next client. It's also a way to set a boundary to value my time as well. It's usually not a problem, and my clients are most often on time.

I did have one client who was chronically late, and would ask if we could change the session time to later in the day or the next day or would arrive twenty or even thirty minutes late. We talked about it, and she seemed aware it was part of a larger pattern in her life of deferring to others' needs at the expense of her own. For example, she would take a business call and not say she needed to leave to be on time to an appointment. I continue to see this client, and she is now much more likely to arrive on time. It's been interesting to see how her boundaries with being on time, as well as her relationships with her family, her partner, and her business partner, have changed in positive ways.

I know other practitioners who will extend the session if they don't have another client right after. As a new practitioner, it's about finding the time boundaries that work for you. Again, as Gary Strauss mentions, often it's best to have stricter boundaries when you're starting out, letting them soften as you become more experienced in your practice. The strict structure gives you a container to work with as you grow and develop your own boundaries.

Cancellation policies

Different practitioners handle cancellations differently. I have a twenty-four-hour cancellation policy, and I post it everywhere: on my website, in my emails, and on my voicemail, and I also tell clients when they book by phone. I also send clients a reminder two days before their appointment to give them plenty of time to cancel or reschedule if they need to.

Contrary to what I've said about softening boundaries over time, I've actually become *more* strict with this policy over the years. When I'm fully booked, and I have a waiting list, it's not fair to have appointments go to waste when there are other clients who want to see me and I don't have an available opening.

It's also not fair to me as the practitioner—I'm setting aside my time for the client, and I want them to respect my time. I charge for a missed appointment or a last-minute cancellation, unless it's a true emergency. Occasionally if it's a long-time or a really good client, I'll charge fifty percent or make a one-time exception for a nonemergency no-show or last-minute cancellation, depending on the circumstances.

Other practitioners are more lax about this—one practitioner I know feels that when a client cancels, it's usually a signal that he could use a little extra rest. But for me it's important to set the boundary that my time is valuable, as valuable as my clients', and I want them to respect this principle, as well as ensure that clients that really want a session will be able to get one.

Gary Strauss takes a big-picture perspective on cancellations—if a client reschedules or cancels three times in a row, he won't work with that client in the future. It's not something he tells clients in advance, and it's not something he gets upset about; it's just his policy.

Dealing with difficult clients

First of all, the word "difficult" can have varying definitions, so I always check in with myself when dealing with a client who isn't easy to see if I'm being emotionally triggered by whatever is challenging about this person. This helps me figure out how best to handle the situation and interact with the client.

For example, if they're difficult in the sense that they're always late or they don't show up or they don't really seem interested in getting better, then I handle them by letting them go lightly. (I give you an example of the kind of language I use below.) This idea of letting them go lightly is an idea I got from Joanna Crespo. The premise is that you don't push back on the client by getting angry, or talking strongly about their unwanted behavior. Instead, you just let them go lightly, which is easier to do than describe. You're not forcing, you're not getting upset, you're in as neutral a mind-set as possible. In other words, you're not pushing your agenda on them, you're allowing them to be as they are and gently let them know that you think another practitioner or type of work might be a better fit for them. Part of letting clients go lightly is about truly believing that there are plenty of people out there who need what you do, and plenty of therapists whose practice may fit a particular need that you simply don't want to serve.

If I'm really triggered by somebody, then I know there's something on my end that I need to work on. This becomes a good growth opportunity for me to practice remaining as neutral as possible in my interactions with the client, and not get charged by them if they're unpleasant or demanding. I sometimes seek additional help from various resources—talking to a colleague or mentor, getting a session for myself, etc.

I also sometimes get clients who are unpleasant and demanding, but whose behavior doesn't particularly bother me. Yes, it's wonderful to have pleasant and easygoing clients, but if I'm not thinking about how they acted or what they said repeatedly in my mind, then I'm not triggered by their behavior. And when it does bother me, I think, okay, what's on my end that I need to attend to or work on?

With this kind of work, you will be forced to face your own issues, which is why it's so important to have some kind of daily meditation practice and to find ways to take care of yourself. I'll talk about this more later on in the book.

Firing a client

I've only fired one client in my years of practice, so I don't think this is going to be something that you deal with often, but it's worth addressing. It's also a good example of how to be neutral in the face of challenging client behaviors.

This client came to me for one session, then missed three sessions after that, cancelling thirty minutes beforehand. She rescheduled a few more times, but still didn't make it to her appointments. She was also reluctant to pay for the missed appointments.

We spoke on the phone, and then I followed up with an email saying that because of her busy work schedule and my limited availability (she needed evening appointments, and at this stage in my practice those tended to book up a month or more in advance), I felt another practitioner with a more flexible schedule, or who worked later hours, might be a better fit for her. I also said I wouldn't charge her for this missed appointment. It was quite civilized, and I think it helped that I wasn't worked up or upset, I just wanted to be clear that this didn't seem to be working for either of us, and to stop trying to force it to work.

Other times I've been up front with a client that maybe a different practitioner, or a different kind of bodywork or therapy, might be a better fit. I do this if either the client or I doesn't see the client getting results. For example, I had a client with severe insomnia. I've worked with many clients who found hypnosis extremely beneficial for helping them sleep better. However, this client came for five hypnosis sessions, but wasn't seeing improvement. He liked the hypnosis sessions and found them quite relaxing, but he wasn't sleeping any better. I suggested that while I would be happy to continue seeing him, it seemed like it might be time to try something else. He seemed surprised, and very appreciative of my honesty—previously he'd gone for ten or fifteen acupuncture sessions without seeing improvement, and he'd been the one to end the treatment.

I also had a client with an intense boundary issue. He'd been through a lot. He'd been a victim of satanic ritual abuse—not my normal client, nor my area of expertise. Because of this, I insisted on talking to his therapist, just to make sure that it was the right time for him to be getting energy work. I told him: "I want to make sure that I have your wellbeing in mind, and my own." I did know that with trauma there are different phases in the psychiatric treatment process, and I wanted to make sure a session wouldn't trigger anything that the client wouldn't be able to handle.

The client didn't want me to talk to his therapist, but I insisted—nicely. I finally spoke to the therapist, and the therapist confirmed that he had severe boundary and trust issues, which of course made sense, given his past. The therapist didn't feel there should be a problem with treatment, but as it happened, this client didn't come back for a session, which was fine. I didn't think we were a great fit, and I did think it was important for me to set a boundary for myself and him. So I didn't fire him, he quit on his own, but this is also an example of how to let go of a client lightly.

Again, these are two examples that are quite out of the ordinary, but I want you to be prepared and have some ideas of how to handle various situations that may come your way.

Homework: Deciding how to handle challenging clients

Consider the following questions:

- What is your cancellation policy?
- What is your policy for clients who are late to their appointments?
- Who can you call on for support/guidance when dealing with client challenges?
- What kind of self-care will give you support when dealing with challenging client situations?

14

Establishing Administrative Practices

It's so important to stay organized—you work more efficiently and spend less time on administrative tasks, client relationships are smoother, and it frees up time for you to enjoy your work, as well as your personal life. In this chapter, I'll show you how to set up the administrative aspects of your practice—such as client booking, intake forms, and client files—as well as how to deal with financial management, such as taxes, invoicing, and credit cards.

Booking

I was surprised to find that the majority of my clients now contact me by email—not many prospective clients call me to book an appointment. This may not be true for you, especially depending on the average age of your clients—for example, the majority of my clients are between the ages of twenty and forty, so this may explain their indifference to the phone.

As a result, I used to spend a lot of time emailing clients back and forth to schedule sessions. This was fine in the beginning, but three years ago I switched to an online booking system with a monthly subscription fee. (If you want recommendations, go to the Business Starter Kit on my website.)

I've been really happy with it. It connects with QuickBooks (my accounting software—more on this later), offers useful reports to help me analyze my business, sends all sorts of customizable automated emails (for example, as mentioned in the previous chapter, it sends a reminder email to my clients two days before their session). It offers different settings so you can modify and personalize it according to your needs. Clients can't see my schedule—they only see available openings, and there are ways for you to personalize this as well. The customer service for my online booking tool is among the best I've ever experienced—they are super-responsive and helpful.

Now, I don't think you necessarily need a service like this in the beginning. When I saw five clients a month, I didn't need an online booking system. But when I started seeing five to ten clients a week, it was really useful. It also helps you look more professional. If you don't need an online booking system, make sure you set up a good calendar system, because you need one that's going to help you keep track of sessions and stay organized. Also, think about if you want to remind your clients of their upcoming appointments by phone, email, text, etc.

Intake form

You probably received a sample intake form during your training. If not, I've included a sample intake form in the Business Starter Kit on my website. You'll want to personalize it depending on your services and specialty.

In my intake form, I ask if the client is currently on medication or under psychiatric care. If they are, I ask to speak to their doctor or their psychiatrist if their health condition is not under control, or if I need additional clarification. I explain to the client that I'm part of their treatment team, and I want to make sure that other members of their team are aware of what I'm doing and vice versa—I want to get advice from them to make sure I'm supporting the client as best I can, and not going outside my scope of practice. With hypnosis clients, I definitely want a medical referral if they are coming for help with reducing pain, because pain can be an indication that something else is going on that needs to be checked out by a doctor.

I like my clients to fill out the intake form before their session, so they can start thinking about how they want to change and what support they want from the session. I email it to them in advance once they've booked an appointment. Some hypnotists prefer that the client fill it out in person, or prefer to ask the form's questions aloud, so they can observe verbal and nonverbal responses that may help them personalize the session.

Disclaimer

I have clients sign a disclaimer at the end of the intake form. This is something you should develop with the advice of an attorney, and get specific advice for your practice. Basically it's a statement saying you are not a doctor, you don't diagnose illness or prescribe treatment, and the client should seek medical attention if needed.

Client files

I have a locked filing cabinet where I keep all my clients' intake forms. Sometimes I make notes on individual files, or I keep notes in an Excel document (again, check out the Business Starter Kit on my website for a template you can use). Legally, you need to ensure client confidentiality by keeping files under lock and key.

Forms of payment

I didn't accept credit cards when I first started my practice, but this was before all the card readers that are available now that allow you to use your smartphone to charge credit cards.

You might want to start out by keeping it simple and accepting only cash and checks, and once you get more clients, you can move to accepting credit cards. On the other hand, so many people use credit cards, and the convenience and ease of use for your clients is a nice thing to be able to offer.

One thing to take into consideration is that the various card-reader services take a small deduction from each payment as a service charge. These charges are deductible business expenses for tax purposes. You can choose whether or not to actively pass this fee on to the client, although I personally don't, and don't recommend it. Your client demographic is also worth considering—younger clients are more used to using credit cards for everything, while some of my older clients still prefer to use checks, or pay in cash.

I also use PayPal on my website for people who want to purchase a gift certificate for a friend or loved one. Again, my advice is to keep it simple while you're starting out; you can always offer more options later as your business expands.

15

Handling Money

Let's move on to setting your fees and charging clients.

Setting your fees

Figuring out what to charge clients is definitely not a black-or-white process. I recommend three important steps.

- Research: Start by researching other practitioners in your town or city to get a lay of the land. When I first did this, I quickly realized some practitioners charged a lot, and others very little, but I was able to get an estimated median rate.
- Evaluate: The next step is to evaluate your experience level. If you're just starting out, you're probably going to charge less than someone who's been practicing for twenty years. As I previously mentioned, I remember one of my teachers telling me that new practitioners should do at least a hundred sessions for free before they start charging clients. I make this recommendation to my Reiki III students, too, so that they have a solid foundation and comfort level in working with people. Once you're ready to charge

as a professional practitioner, you want to feel comfortable dealing with whatever situation may arise. Dealing with unexpected situations is a part of having your own practice (and life!), but a certain baseline level of experience will serve you well, helping you stay grounded no matter what comes up in a session.

+ Calculate: The final and most important step in figuring out what to charge is to calculate how much you need to make a living. This exercise yielded very surprising results for me. I'll provide a worksheet in the Business Starter Kit on my website to help you figure out how many sessions you can realistically do in a week, how many weeks you plan to work per year, etc., to give you a sense of what you'll need to earn to take care of yourself financially. I'll also go into more detail in the next chapter.

When I was first starting my practice, I did my research and assessed what I needed to make, and then I came up with a rate. It felt like a stretch, so I usually offered $10 off a client's first session. I increased my rates over the years as I gained more experience.

I've changed my rates three times over the past seven years. Every time I increase my rates, I pick a number that feels right to me. I tend to be intuitive with numbers, which might sound a little strange, but once I did the three steps listed above as a benchmark, that's how I've done it ever since.

I remember initially thinking—and this was in 2008 in New York City—that $100 an hour was probably a great living. But once I filled out something similar to the worksheet I'm posting on my website, I had a rude awakening. Here are some of the costs I hadn't taken into consideration initially:

+ As a practitioner working in New York City, I needed to set aside approximately 35 percent of my income for taxes.
+ I needed to deduct my office space rental and other related expenses.

- I needed to account for time spent with each client beyond the session, and for pre- and post-session preparations:
  - Reserving space, if you share the treatment room with other practitioners
  - Prep time—speaking on the phone or emailing with clients to schedule a session, answering any questions the client might have, etc.
  - Follow-up time—taking down treatment notes following the session, answering any follow-up questions the client might have, etc.
  - Setting up and cleaning up the treatment room
- Time spent on administrative and marketing tasks—about twenty hours or more per week that is unpaid.

Once I filled out this worksheet, $100 an hour quickly became quite a bit less-lucrative sounding. Hopefully, the worksheet on my website will help you avoid uncomfortable surprises of your own in figuring out your rates.

Money issues

Much has been written on the topic of money issues, and dealing with any negative beliefs you might have around money will help your business thrive. I remember in my Reiki Master program there were several students in my class who were uncomfortable at the thought of charging at all (which makes it difficult to make a living doing this work!).

Practitioners sometimes have trouble dealing with money, worrying that it's not "spiritual" to be concerned about making a living. Reiki teacher and practitioner Frans Stiene speaks to this concern:

"Money is just another form of energy. There are a few strange misconceptions about this, especially in the Reiki community. One is that people need to pay you something in return or give you something back in return, otherwise they won't appreciate your Reiki session. This is a very odd idea.

"One of the precepts within the system of Reiki is 'show compassion to yourself and others.' When we are really compassionate, it doesn't matter what we get or if we get anything at all; we do it because we have compassion, and real compassion doesn't need anything in return.

"I often hear from new practitioners or teachers that 'my client didn't even say thank you!' And they feel very hurt by this. If we practice from this point of view, we are not practicing from true compassion. Plus, if we practice from this viewpoint and we get no feedback we feel hurt, which, in turn, is not good for us as the practitioner.

"Of course, if you set up shop, you need to pay for the rental of the treatment room, your time, brochures, the massage table, etc., so you need to charge your clients, so that you're able to offer a service.

"I also feel that the client is paying you for your expertise, so in fact they kind of pay you to meditate and take your practice deeper so that you can become a clearer vehicle to help them.

"Another concern is that when I say that we all have Reiki within us a client might ask: 'Why do I have to pay for Reiki if I am Reiki already?' Then my answer is: 'Yes, you're right, so why not stand outside and connect to the Reiki within and let the healing take place?'

"But of course they'll answer: 'But I don't know how to do that.'

"My reply: 'That's why you pay me: to help you rediscover your own healing ability.'"

Similarly, hypnosis and NLP teacher and practitioner Sarah Carson discusses the importance of acknowledging the time and effort you've spent in becoming a practitioner, and what the exchange of money means to you and your client:

"When I first started my practice I did not see myself as a business person. I was idealistic but not practical. Unfortunately we see this pattern with many coaches and hypnotists. They want to change lives but they can't pay their rent.

"My attitude changed when a friend said to me 'how can you change the world if you can't afford to eat?' It was like a light bulb went on and I got serious about building a practice.

"Taking the time to recognize the amount of time and money you've spent in your training, and that your time and expertise is incredibly valuable, is important. Another interesting aspect is to understand that when your client is exchanging money for the experience, they'll often have a deeper commitment to the change.

"If we are giving our work away for free, this diminishes the efficacy of the work, and denigrates you and your expertise. Even if you ask for a small amount, then the chances of your work being seen as effective and valuable in your clients' eyes increases tremendously."

Heart-centered business expert Leonie Dawson also has much to say on this topic. (Refer to the Business Starter Kit on my website [www.centertruehealth.com/business-starter-kit] for more information about her.)

Increasing your rates as needed

Even though I've been doing this for many years, anytime I've increased my rates, I've felt a little uncomfortable and nervous about it, and I think that's a good thing, because it's a stretch to grow into charging a higher rate.

Here are three recommendations to help you when it's time to increase your rates:

+ Tell current clients: I make sure to tell my existing clients well in advance that my rates will be increasing. I send them an email and tell them in person to prepare them for the change.
+ Create a special offer: When I still offered packages, I used to tell current clients that they could purchase packages before my rates went up. I chose to have the increase correspond with the calendar year's end. So in October I would say, "I'm raising my rates

in January. You can buy as many packages as you want before the end of the year, and use those sessions next year."

+ Allow for special circumstances: I continued to offer the old rate to a few longtime clients with extenuating circumstances. For example, I have a client who's retired. I worked with him intensively when he was dealing with prostate and colon cancer. Now he comes every now and then for proactive maintenance sessions. I let him know I was increasing my rates, in case he planned to refer new clients to me, but then I let him know I'd like to offer my old rate to him as a special courtesy.

I did lose some clients. I had one or two clients tell me that my rates were too expensive for them. And I learned to be okay with this, particularly because the people that told me this usually weren't my ideal clients (the type of clients I've defined as my niche and who I'm specifically focused on helping).

I think it's important to remind myself from time to time that I'm not the only practitioner out there, and that there are a range of practitioners who can meet lots of different kinds of client needs, including different price points. If they need a less-expensive option, they'll be able to find the right practitioner. In my experience—and other seasoned practitioners have agreed when I've asked them if they've had a similar experience—the clients who ask for discounts and special rates and exceptions often don't need it as much as somebody who might not ask.

Often these "discount clients" aren't my ideal client anyway. They're pushing and testing my boundaries, and it's been good for me to identify and clarify my boundaries around money. In the past, sometimes I did give these clients a discount, but often I didn't feel good about it afterward. Becoming comfortable with your boundaries is an important process, and clients are great at testing areas where you aren't comfortable!

On the flip side, I've also realized that sometimes clients appreciate and value the session more if it is a bit of a financial stretch. Some clients think that the more you charge, the better you are. I remember an acupuncturist and teacher told me about one of her students who had just graduated from acupuncture school, and had only a basic knowledge of acupuncture. This student charged $350 for a one-hour session right out of school, and she wasn't even one of the most promising students, but people went to her because they thought, "Oh, if she's charging that much, she must be good."

This is a pretty extreme example, and no, you probably shouldn't be charging $350 an hour if you just finished your training, but be aware that people value the things in their lives that are hard won. Look at other practitioners, and come up with a fair rate for your town or city that also feels right to you.

I continue to work at becoming comfortable with my own value and the value that I provide to others, and to let go of my insecurities around money and pricing. Be gentle with yourself: the growing pains throughout the process of determining your rates are normal.

Sliding scale and pay-what-you-wish

I don't offer sliding scale or pay-what-you-wish services. I think it's kind of a cop-out, because it's making your client take on the burden of telling you what you're worth, and that puts a weird energetic layer on the relationship. It's also not taking ownership of your needs. Consider it this way: if you're not in a financially stable position with your practice, how can you possibly offer pay-what-you-wish sessions? Each person will need to make this decision for themselves, but I think it's essential to remember that you need to be able to take care of yourself and your financial needs to better be able to take care of others.

I know a practitioner who is just starting her art therapy practice. She's finding it hard to turn away prospective clients if they can't pay her full fee, and offers a sliding scale. At first, she was letting the client suggest a price, and then she would negotiate from there. She quickly realized that this didn't feel good to her, and instead came up with a set reduced rate for clients who couldn't pay her full fee.

Another situation in which offering pay-what-you-wish services might be appropriate is if you're finishing your training and want to start charging. This could help you ease into getting comfortable with charging for sessions, but doesn't leave you dependent on making your living with this income. Keep in mind, though, that most likely clients you meet this way will not continue with you once you start charging your full rate. I think this is fine, because you're going to be at a different level of experience when you do start to charge your full rate, and as you grow as a practitioner, you'll attract a different kind of client.

How to handle prospective clients who say they can't pay your full rate

There are different views on this topic. Some marketing experts think that if you talk to a prospective client and start building a relationship with them, then when you introduce your fee further into the conversation, they're more apt to recognize the value you offer and be more willing to pay it. This, too, is a completely valid assertion—so as always, you'll need to figure out what works best for you.

This hasn't been a huge issue for me, I think because I list my rates on my website. At first, I was hesitant to do this, because when I started my practice I didn't see other practitioners doing this online. Now I see more people listing their rates online, and it has worked well for me.

If a prospective client can't pay my full fee, I'll usually refer them to other practitioners who charge less, or tell them about a clinic setting where students in training offer a discounted rate.

Bear in mind that sometimes when people say something is too expensive, it doesn't necessarily mean "I can't afford it." It just means "it's not worth it to me," which is fine. Not everybody's going to find the same value in what you do. Your job is to find the people who do (as discussed in Chapter 6).

Sometimes—and I don't do this very often—I'll offer a discount for clients who I think or know don't have the financial resources of some of my other clients. This is usually based on a gut feeling, and occasionally I've been wrong, but I usually do it if someone seems very invested in wanting to make positive changes in their life, but simply can't afford my services, and I feel called to do it.

Volunteering and giving back

At some point, ideally once your practice is thriving and you're able to make a living with the work that you do, you can decide to offer free or discounted sessions as a way to give back if you feel called to do so. For example, I used to volunteer offering Reiki in the hospice ward at the hospital. I also think of my current work at NYU Medical this way—it's not financially viable, but it's my way of giving back to lower-income clients.

Getting comfortable handling money

I know for some new practitioners handling money is entirely comfortable. It wasn't for me. Although I was a fundraiser for fifteen years, I wasn't used to asking for money for myself. I was used to asking for lots of money for the nonprofits that I worked for, which is quite different.

Getting comfortable asking for money takes practice—it gets easier the more you do it. I remember my first client. Her name was Hope, which in retrospect I think was auspicious. And working with Hope was the first time I had to ask for money following a session. I used a line that I had memorized, which I highly recommend you do if you're at all nervous about asking for payment. The more you rehearse it, the more comfortable you'll feel as it becomes second nature to say.

At the end of her session, I simply said, "How would you like to pay—cash or check?" I think we can get worked up about asking for payment, but it's actually completing the circle of energy between the client and the practitioner. But it did take practice for me to get comfortable taking the initiative in this completion.

Trading for other services

Over the years, I've had people ask me to do a trade, where I give them a session in exchange for the service they offer. I've done it in a couple of situations, and other times I've said no. This may seem obvious, but it's worth saying: make sure you're actually interested in what the other person is offering you. For example, I have a friend who is a Pilates instructor, and she asked me to do a trade. I think Pilates is great, but I didn't have enough time or interest to want to do a one-for-one trade. So I said no.

In another instance, I did trade with a close friend who was my website designer. This was definitely treading on thin ice, because I didn't want to jeopardize our friendship. We came up with some boundaries and guidelines ahead of time. She's very professional and I pride myself on being professional, too. We tried to be as upfront as possible about what our working relationship would be like and what we both needed. We also each agreed to let the other one know if at any point it wasn't working. We've been working together now for several years, and it's worked out well. In retrospect, I feel like it might have been better to pay each other, because I think this can help you value each other's work more, but in general, the trade has worked well for us.

Astrology coach and spiritual counselor Maria Rodriguez talks about finding the right balance: "I think exchanging services can be great, and I think especially for people starting out, it can help you reduce your costs as you're getting off the ground.

"But I think there needs to be a cap. For something like web design, that takes a certain amount of time to do, I think you have to be upfront about the exchange. For example, 'I'll give you three sessions for X,' so that it's clear."

Maria brings up a good point. I didn't just do an hour-for-hour trade, because my website designer would have ended up with enough sessions to last for the rest of her life! We figured it out project by project. She picked how many sessions she wanted for a given project (for example, ten sessions from me) and then I paid her hourly rate for the remainder of time she spent creating my website.

I also did a trade for help setting up my social media. Years ago, I didn't know how to create a Facebook page (I know, don't laugh!). I had a coworker at the nonprofit where I worked set up my Facebook page and show me the basics, and in return I gave her two sessions. This is another example of a straightforward trade that worked well.

Trading or bartering services can be a good way to get information or help with something that you don't know how to do, and the person helping you gets a service in return. You just need to make sure the trade is something you both actually need or want, that it's with someone you feel comfortable working with, and that you're clear about the expectations and terms of the trade up front.

It is important to understand that bartering is a cashless exchange of a service or property and the agreed upon fair-market value of the service should be reported as income. Barter as income is defined by the IRS. The expenses related to your barter transactions may be deductible as legitimate business expenses.

Homework: Setting your fees and figuring out your policies

+ Using the steps outlined above, figure out your hourly rate.
+ What are your policies regarding clients who can't pay your full rate?
+ Are you comfortable trading for your services? If so, do you know anyone who offers services for which you might trade?

16

Budgeting

Now that you have some ideas about what to charge and how to handle issues that may come up with clients around money, let's focus on getting your financial systems in place. How to do what you love while still being able to make a living is a major concern I hear over and over again from new (and seasoned!) practitioners. I've been there myself.

I'm going to share what I've gleaned over the years to help you manage your money and the financial aspects of your practice in a heart-centered way. I'll give you templates to modify and make your own, which you can use to create a budget and manage cash flow.

Creating a budget

Putting together a budget is the first step in building the financial foundation of your practice. In the Business Starter Kit on my website I've given you a sample budget for income and expenses you can use.

To keep track of my income, I created an Excel spreadsheet that includes:

- Date and time of the service
- Name of the client
- How much the client paid for the session
- Form of payment (cash, check, credit card)
- Client notes
- The total income for each month

For expenses, we'll get a little help from my mom, who's experienced in account management and tax preparation for sole proprietors. When I first started my practice, she explained to me the IRS expense categories for businesses. I still use these categories for tracking my expenses, with a few modifications, because as a wellness practitioner I have different expenses than other businesses (for example, linen cleanings, a massage table, hypnosis chair, etc.).

Once you've tracked your income and expenses for a full year, you'll have data to reference when creating your budget projections for the next year. You'll also need this information to do your taxes—more on this in a bit. Because you'll have information from past years, budgeting gets easier over time. You'll also start noticing when the busier and slower times of year tend to occur, and this information will help you manage cash flow.

Cash flow

Speaking of cash flow—what is it? Good question. I never realized how important it was until I started my own business. Cash flow is the movement of money in and out of your business over a given time period. It's all about timing.

For example, you might have a large expense due on a certain date, but you may have income coming in at a later date. Now, as the owner of your practice, you'll likely receive payment the day the client comes to see you for a session. Unlike many other small business owners, you probably won't submit invoices and then need to wait for payment. This makes things easier; you get paid the day you perform the service.

However, if you partner with other organizations, you may need to submit invoices for your services and get paid at a later date. For example, the hospital where I work pays me ninety days after I submit my invoice for seeing patients.

You might also incur certain expenses in advance of receiving payment. For example, you might need to buy a massage table or a hypnosis chair before you start seeing clients. Managing cash flow has been a major challenge for me as I built my practice, because for fifteen years I was used to receiving a steady paycheck from a full-time job. Not being able to count on a set monthly income has made it hard to figure out how much to set aside for upcoming quarterly payments of state and federal taxes, and even to make a basic plan for my personal finances. Because it's been a struggle for me, I want to give you templates to help you avoid what I've gone through and help you figure out how to navigate cash flow. The good news: if you're already comfortable doing freelance work, or some kind of job where the income varies from month to month, this won't be as difficult for you.

As I project my income for each month, I take into consideration various factors: if I'm going to be out of town at any point during the month or if I'm planning to take a class and won't have as many available days to see clients, or if it's summer and I'm doing fewer sessions because clients are out of town or on vacation, etc.

But the projection is just a projection, as with any kind of budgeting. Think of it as a road map: it offers directions on how to get there, but it can't tell you if there's going to be more or less traffic than usual. It might be faster or slower to get there one day versus another, even though you're traveling the same route. Clients cancel, or you get sick, and you quickly learn not to count on your projection 100 percent, because life happens. But this budget projection will be a guide to help you. (And hey, this isn't a bad principle to apply to your work with clients—you can have ideas about what you're going to do during a client session, but while it's good to have a plan, things will always come up and you'll need to flow with it!)

The importance of planning ahead

Planning is key. I didn't do it in the beginning when I was first setting up my practice. (I wish I had.) Now I realize the importance of creating a budget with specific goals. I'm doing it even more strategically the past couple of years than I have in the past, thanks to Leonie Dawson's Business Academy (Check out the Business Starter Kit on my website to find out more about Leonie; her membership program has been the best investment I've made in my business, hands down. Plus, she's an amazing and inspiring person, and we all need more people like that in our lives.)

Establishing concrete monthly goals helps me set my intentions and stay focused on what I need to do to achieve them. Monthly goals with corresponding action steps will help you stay on track, without becoming overwhelmed. This is one of the most important things you can do to build a thriving practice.

17

Organizing Your Money

Even if you don't love managing money, keeping organized about it is a form of doing self-care and investing in your success. In this chapter, I'll offer several strategies and suggestions for you to try. Be willing to experiment and find the strategies for tracking income and expenses that work for you—and remember, any strategy that you'll use consistently and carefully to track where your money goes is better than not having a strategy at all.

Income & expenses

Again, I'll give you a template of Excel spreadsheets you can use to track your income and expenses in the Business Starter Kit on my website, but here are some examples of the basic income-tracking categories you can use:

- Client sessions (organized by date, name of client, amount paid, and payment method)
- Gift certificates (organized by date, name of purchaser, name of recipient, amount paid, payment method, date redeemed)
- Partners (for example, if you work for a hospital, organized by

date, amount paid, date payment was received if you aren't paid the day you work)

Here are some examples of the deductible expense categories you can use:

+ Advertising (business cards, marketing, and printing costs)
+ Credit card fees (PayPal, Square, etc.)
+ Office expenses (postage and office supplies)
+ Rent for office space
+ Phone/Internet
+ Travel and deductible meals
+ Website design and hosting
+ Professional journals and membership fees
+ Continuing education

Earlier, I mentioned how I keep my receipts in an accordion file folder—I have a tab for each of the categories listed above and keep receipts in the corresponding folder—most recent receipt in the front of each folder.

Checking account

Soon after I started seeing clients, I opened a separate personal checking account; I still use it. It's not a business account, but it keeps the money from my business separate from my personal funds. Ask your bank or your accountant for their recommendations on what kind of account to establish, because this will vary by state and country, and by your personal situation. The most important thing is to keep your business finances separate from your personal finances. (The IRS frowns on commingling your money!)

Accounting software

Quickbooks is an accounting software package for small business owners. I started using it last year, although it had been on my to-do list for a couple of years. I bought the software a year before I finally started using it. This is a great example of how some things take time to get going, so you need to find that balance between being gentle with yourself to allow time to implement new things, and also staying focused so you get your business up and running.

I didn't really need Quickbooks for the first couple of years in my business, but I could have used it sooner than last year. Quickbooks streamlines your financial tracking and makes it easier to do your taxes. It's easier for my accountant and my bookkeeper, which means they spend less time preparing my taxes, and as a result I save money.

I mention Quickbooks so you have an idea of where you're headed. In the meantime, you can use the Excel document that I'll give you in the Business Starter Kit on my website (www.centertruehealth.com/business-starter-kit). This document will keep you organized. And when you need a more robust tracking system, you can think about Quickbooks (or another kind of small-business accounting software). For a couple of years before I started using Quickbooks, I felt like I was trying to create my own database to organize my income and expenses. I'll give you something basic to start with that will help you keep track of cash flow in a simple way.

Savings and retirement accounts

I wasn't able to set aside anything for savings or retirement when I was first starting out with my practice. It was a sacrifice I had to make if I wanted to start my own business. It was a little depressing, because over the past five years in my full-time job I had finally been able to really focus on building my savings and retirement funds.

In the second and third years of my business, I was able to save a small monthly amount. Setting up an automatic monthly deduction from my checking account into my savings account helped me make sure that I was saving something, even though it was much less than I'd been saving when I had a full-time office job.

A couple of years ago I was able to create a SEP account. According to the U.S. Department of Labor, a Simplified Employee Pension (SEP) plan allows you to set aside money for yourself in a traditional individual retirement account. It allows for a contribution of up to 25 percent of your income, it's tax deductible, and you aren't locked into making contributions every year. Basically, it's an IRA (individual retirement account) for people who have their own business. Again, you're going to want to discuss this with an accountant in more detail.

Homework: Organizing your money

- Using the budget template I give you in the Business Starter Kit on my website, come up with a list of your income and expense categories.
- Set a date to have a draft budget completed so you make sure you get it done. You can make modifications as you start using it and develop a better sense of what you need to track.
- Figure out if you can set aside money in a savings account on a monthly basis, and if so, set it up so it's automated.

18

Finding Financial Support

Getting the financial systems of your business in place may feel a little overwhelming, but of course, you're not alone, because you can (and should) get expert help such as an accountant, bookkeeper, and lawyer to guide you.

Accountants

If you don't have experience with running your own business, and you've previously worked in a completely different field, it's especially helpful to find a good accountant.

When I first started my practice, I asked around but didn't find a good accountant right away. And in retrospect, during this time I was only seeing approximately four clients a month. It wasn't a lot. So I was able to ease into getting an accountant. Ideally you want to find an expert who can help you navigate getting your financial systems, taxes, and legal responsibilities established.

Having an accountant is a huge help because as a business owner, my tax return is more complex than when I was working full-time and receiving a W2 form—not to mention the fact that New York State taxes are notoriously complicated. Having an accountant is a great resource—I can check in with him around November to see if my annual income projections are on target, and to see if my quarterly tax payments need to be adjusted. The IRS penalizes you for not paying enough if your income exceeds the projection you gave them at the beginning of the year. This is why you want to check in with your accountant.

Bookkeepers

I didn't get a bookkeeper until last year, but I think it's helpful to have one once you're seeing more than thirty clients a month. If you're just starting out and only seeing a few clients, you don't need a bookkeeper, but as your business gains momentum, getting financial components in place with professional help will keep you organized and streamline your business. Plus, it allows you more time to see clients and do the work you love. I work with my bookkeeper remotely, and she spends a few hours once a month reconciling my checking and credit card statement expenses and entering client income from sessions and classes in Quickbooks.

Legal stuff

When starting your own business, you need to decide what form of business entity to establish. This determines what kind of income tax return you need to file, and it's important for additional tax and legal reasons. This is something you'll *definitely* want to discuss with an accountant and/or a lawyer, because these issues will vary by state and your personal situation. But here's a brief overview of your options, taken from the IRS website. (If you live in another country, skip this section and find an accountant or lawyer where you live who can advise you.)

The most common forms of business for wellness practitioners are sole proprietor, LLC, and S corporation.

Sole Proprietor:

A sole proprietor is someone who owns an unincorporated business by him or herself. Since I'm a sole proprietor, I have a separate personal checking account for my business rather than a business account. If you end up creating an LLC or an S corporation—and this is probably further down the line, once your practice is more established—you would need to open a business checking account. As a sole proprietor you will file a Schedule C or Schedule C-EZ with your 1040 tax forms.

As a sole proprietor, you also do not have the legal protection of being an LLC or an S corporation. If a sole proprietor is sued for some reason by a client or vendor, his or her personal assets (which could include things like a home, a car, a retirement account, emergency savings, and so forth) as well as the assets of the business would be vulnerable to reclamation as part of any legal remedy ordered by the court.

Limited Liability Company (LLC):

LLCs vary slightly by state, so check your state's tax code. Basically, though, unlike a sole proprietorship, an LLC is an entity separate from you—it's a company, not a person.

S corporation:

An S corporation is a corporation that elects to pass corporate income, losses, deductions, and credits through to its shareholders for federal tax purposes. Shareholders of S corporations report the flow-through of income and losses on their personal tax returns, and are assessed tax at their individual income tax rates. This allows S corporations to avoid double taxation on corporate income.

I think 90 percent of people starting out with their practice will want to form a sole proprietorship, which keeps things simple. As your business grows, you might look into becoming an LLC or an S corporation. Again, you should absolutely discuss this with an accountant or lawyer. In the Business Starter Kit on my website, I'll give you additional resources to help you with this process.

Paying taxes

Yes, I know, talking about taxes is probably not at the top of your list of fun things to do, believe me I can relate, but I'm going to make it as clear and simple as possible.

As the owner of your own business, you aren't receiving a paycheck from an employer with your taxes already deducted, so you'll need to pay quarterly taxes to the IRS. You will need to pay federal taxes based on your net income after expenses and your filing status. Refer to the IRS tax table. The IRS also accesses SE or a self-employment tax on your net self-employment income. The FICA taxes are your contribution to social security and Medicare. The SE rate is a percentage of net self-employment income.

If you wait until the end of the year to pay your taxes, the IRS adds a penalty fee to your balance due. To avoid this, you need to pay quarterly estimated taxes. The IRS wants you to look into your crystal ball and predict what your income will be for the year. They also have a special definition of "quarterly." Due dates for estimated tax payments are April 15, June 15, September 15, and January 15. Note that these "quarterly" dates are not every 3 months, which drives me a little crazy.

I was quite surprised when I learned about quarterly taxes. I still find dealing with them somewhat challenging, but when I first started my practice, it really threw me, because it was difficult to figure out how much I needed to set aside each month, especially with the unique definition of quarterly—sometimes I have four months to set aside money for my next quarterly payment, while other times I have two months. That's a big difference!

It didn't help that my first accountant *really* overestimated my payments. I was struggling to set money aside, and I even asked her to double check, and she said the amounts she told me were correct. The following year, I changed accountants and I didn't owe any taxes for the upcoming year because I had paid so much the previous year. That gives you a sense of how much I overpaid!

Again, the budget spreadsheet I include in the Business Starter Kit on my website will help you project your income for the year, and a good accountant will be able to guide you as you plan your quarterly taxes.

Homework: Get financial support

- Ask friends and family for recommendations for a good accountant and/or bookkeeper if you don't already have one.
- Once you have an accountant, figure out what type of business entity to establish and set up a separate checking account for your business.
- With your accountant's help, figure out your quarterly tax payments.

19

How to Avoid Burnout

Figuring out ways to avoid getting burned out is a common concern among wellness practitioners, and figuring out a schedule that works for you is key. As I've said before, your schedule will evolve over time as you grow as a practitioner and gain clarity about your needs.

When I had a full-time office job, the set workday of 9:30 a.m. to 6:30 p.m. gave me a solid structure, even though I often worked longer hours. Having my own practice, my schedule is much more flexible, which is a huge plus, and something I really love about having my own business. But it's much harder for me to end the work day, and I often work weekends and early mornings on administrative tasks and upcoming projects—this is a huge downside. I'm still working on finding balance between work time and downtime.

When you're first starting your practice, especially if you have a bridge job or some other kind of work to support yourself, it will take extra time to get your new business up and running. This is something to take into consideration as you're getting started. As you figure out a schedule that works for you, here are some suggestions and things to consider:

+ Consider having a set time when you "turn off"—for example, maybe you don't do work in the hour before bed, or maybe Sundays are reserved for downtime.
+ Figure out when you work best. For example, I prefer doing administrative work and writing in the mornings, and like seeing clients later in the day.
+ Think about what you need to take care of yourself (more on this in the next chapter).
+ Some people find it helpful to schedule in their downtime on their calendar as if it's a real appointment.

Playtime

Ok, this is *definitely* one I'm still working on, but it is oh-so important. Truth be told, I used to feel guilty if I even took an hour to read a novel instead of doing something to move my business forward. A couple years ago, I finally realized that if I read a novel for an hour, I usually feel a huge shift in my mood, and it's such an easy (and fun!) way for me to revitalize. Going to the gym or taking a Pilates or yoga class several times a week are other ways for me to take a break from my business, and my body and mind feel better for it.

Astrology coach and spiritual counselor Maria Rodriguez puts it this way:

"This can be hard when you first start out, but I think it's vital to set aside time to do something you love that's unrelated to your business—even if it's once a month, or every other week. For example, I do pottery, which has nothing to do with my work. And it's so wonderful—I'm not answering phones or checking emails for three hours once a week, and it really gives me time to decompress, relax, and connect with myself.

"It's part of your own wellness. It's *you*. If you don't take care of yourself, then how good are you going to be to your clients?"

* * *

Similarly, Thai massage therapist and coach Pamela Herrick shares what helps her avoid burnout:

"Clearly recognizing how many hours of work I can do physically and emotionally has been my most effective way to stay healthy and avoid burnout. I also have a daily meditation practice, and I spend a lot of time in my garden. It is the most grounding and healing part of my day (apart from working with clients).

"Attending classes like yoga or Pilates has never much appealed to me. I dance in the living room with my son (who is eight years old) to wacky music like "Rock Lobster," and we air-guitar a lot. Keeps me normal-ish!"

Integrative hypnosis practitioner and trainer Melissa Tiers finds ways within her work to avoid burnout:

"Even now, after fifteen years as a practitioner, I still go to at least four trainings a year. I think the most exciting thing about this mind field is that it keeps expanding. With every new research study, every shift in neuroscience and mind/body medicine, we get to create new interventions. I think we are so lucky to be at the cutting edge of consciousness. I actively seek aha moments in my work every day. And I'm happy to say, I usually find them."

And Gary Strauss offers another perspective:

"Any time you do the same thing, it becomes repetitive after a while so I think burnout is part of the cycle of life and not necessarily something you need to avoid. You want to go through it and honor the end of a cycle and pattern and move into a new one, a new way of doing this work. Life is a series of adjustments and it will make your work better."

Taking sick days

The first time I had a cold and had to cancel client sessions really threw me. It brought up a big issue for me—the lack of financial stability in having my own business. If I don't work, I don't get paid. Again, coming from a full-time office job, this was something I hadn't dealt with before. Also, I felt keenly the uncertainty of not knowing how many days I would need to take off.

I also had a belief that because I help people find balance and take care of their health, I shouldn't be getting sick. I've heard from many seasoned practitioners that this is a huge trigger for them, especially when they're faced with bigger health challenges, like cancer. This is something you'll work through in your own way, and a good reason to have a strong support network, which I discuss in the next chapter.

Vacation

Vacation is a more fun version but a similar situation to being sick—not getting paid if you're not working. In the past, I've tended to see more clients than usual in a week before and after vacation to make up for lost income while I'm taking time off.

Other practitioners set money aside each month to cover time missed during vacation as well as vacation expenses. It's another consideration to include as you put together your projected budget of income and expenses for the year.

Homework: Finding balance between work and play

+ Write down three steps you can take to set parameters for your work and play time as you find the right work/life balance for you.
+ Name three things you like to do for fun that you can schedule in your weekly or monthly schedule.
+ Think about how you want to handle vacation and sick days.

20

Being True to You

So far I've given you tips for the logistics of starting your wellness practice, from client building and heart-centered marketing to administrative and financial logistics. I've saved the best for last: being true to yourself. This section also builds on the previous chapter, helping you avoid getting burned out.

Many of us learn about being true to ourselves in our various trainings to become healing arts practitioners, but it bears repeating because it's so important. What's the best way to ensure that you'll be able to have a successful and thriving wellness practice, working with lovely clients who need and value your help and expertise, with enough income to take care of your needs, without getting burned out? It's to be true to yourself, and figure out what you need to do on a regular basis to take care of yourself.

Now, this is not just a bunch of woo-woo advice. What do I mean by being true to yourself?

Walk your talk

As a practitioner, you're the expert in the client/practitioner relationship. That's why your clients are coming to you for support, guidance, and help. *Follow the advice you give your clients.* What are some of the best pieces of advice or guidance you give your clients? Are you following them yourself? We can't expect our clients to do the work to make positive changes if we aren't willing to follow our own advice. If you got it, use it, right?

I know many practitioners (myself included at times!) who are great at taking care of their clients, but aren't taking care of themselves. What do you need to do to walk your walk? What beliefs do you need to rid yourself of, or acquire, to take your own expert advice?

Receiving wellness services

Polarity teacher and practitioner Gary Strauss gave me this idea years ago, and it's one of my favorite pieces of advice. It's such a great way to take care of yourself: receive a wellness session from another practitioner every week.

Again, as practitioners, we're so busy taking care of others, as well as dealing with the responsibilities of owning our own businesses, that sometimes it's easy to forget to take care of ourselves. What an amazing habit to invest an hour in yourself once a week to reap all the benefits you're already familiar with from the work that you do.

For the most part, I get a wellness session every week, and I noticed a big difference after I started doing this. I get sessions from my mentors, my teachers, and practitioners whose work I value. It helps me work through my own issues—the less "stuff" I have, the more my clients benefit, and the more I can enjoy my life. Getting regular sessions also helps me better deal with clients' energy and challenges. It's also an effective way to develop a support network, which I'll talk more about in the next chapter.

Here's more from Gary Strauss on the subject:

"There's a way to know your work from the inside out, and receiving it changes the way you give it, because it gives you innate intelligence references. I think it's so important to have that reference. Also, without receiving the work, your body and being will be stale. As practitioners, we have to have different ways to open our energies and process our lives on a regular basis."

Now as a Reiki teacher and practitioner, reflexologist and hypnotist, I love receiving all of these kinds of services. But I don't limit my weekly sessions to just these modalities. I get polarity, regular and Thai massage, acupuncture, colonics, homeopathy, etc. I find it fascinating to explore and receive different kinds of healing arts.

And don't let money limit you. Some weeks I'll listen to a hypnosis recording, or do a trade with another practitioner. Be creative. Maybe you prefer every other week. See what works for you.

Meditation and mindfulness practice

As a Reiki teacher and practitioner, having a spiritual practice is a major component of the work that I do. I asked Reiki teacher and practitioner Frans Stiene his perspective on why developing a meditation or spiritual practice is necessary to wellness practitioners. His response:

"Having your own personal spiritual practice is the most important element of any practitioner or teacher, no matter if we are a Reiki teacher, a hypnotist, an acupuncturist, a massage therapist, etc. Why is this?

"Because dealing with your clients is not always that easy. Sticking a needle in someone is in fact not that difficult, and the same can be said of the laying on of hands with Reiki. But dealing with your clients' stuff—this is the hardest thing to do.

"One other element is that we often have the idea that we 'give' a treatment or a teaching. On a very subtle level, when we 'give' something, we feel we have given something away and therefore we have less of whatever we have given.

"The deeper we go within our own personal spiritual practice, the more we start to realize that in reality we are not 'giving' anything at all, we just Be. This is a very important element, because the more we can just Be, the easier it will be to deal with your clients.

"Of course it's also very important to go deeper yourself so that you can take your client deeper. For example, we can say we just stick needles in a client according to what the book says, or we can do hands-on healing on someone according to some standard hand positions, but this is in fact a very basic healing.

"Real deep healing comes from when we see each client as an individual, and therefore we treat each client accordingly. But to really see each client's individual issues we need to first delve deep into our own spiritual nature, so that we can start to go beyond our ego and start to see things clearer: the very essence of things."

I've found that meditating right before I see my first client of the day gets me into the space I need to be in to see clients. It connects me to my intuition (more on this below), helps me let go of judgment and be open, and as Frans says, helps me let go to some extent, of this idea of "giving" a session.

I also found that I needed to figure out what kind of meditation works best for me. I first started out years ago going to a local Zen center and sitting for thirty minutes. While of course this is extremely useful, I've found that taking time for shorter and more frequent meditation (sometimes just a couple of minutes) helps me more. This is also one reason I was drawn to Reiki, because the meditations I learned in my Reiki classes really resonated with me. My husband meditates by listening to music—he's completely focused and quiets his mind, attuned to the present moment. So remember that there's no right or wrong, it's finding out what works for you.

Developing your intuition

Your intuition is your biggest asset in working with clients and growing your practice. The more you use it, the stronger it gets; it's a skill, like anything else. It's the best tool I know to help you make the right decisions for your business (not to mention your life)—to do what feels right, not what you think you should do or what someone told you to do.

As I continue to work with clients, meditate, and work on myself by getting sessions, taking classes, and so forth, my intuition becomes stronger.

Love what you do

One thing that will help your meditation and strengthen your intuition is to keep what you love to do front and center. It's a kind of meditation to always bring yourself back, reminding yourself: "I love to do it, these are the things I love about it, and I'm so grateful I get to do this work."

Starting your own business is hard work, and takes perseverance, focus, and discipline. The more you can stay centered on what you love about this work, the better.

How can you remind yourself of the things you love about your work? An affirmation that resonates with you, taped to your desk? A gratitude jar that you add to weekly? Taking a few moments as you're falling asleep to reflect on the wonderful moments, no matter how small, that you experienced that day involving your practice or something else in your life?

These are some of the things I like to do—what else inspires you?

On the subject of having the right mind-set to do work you love, Reiki teacher and practitioner Joanna Crespo puts it best:

"Have fun and let go. This is a quote I really like: 'Worrying is like praying for what you don't want.'"

Homework: Developing a mindfulness practice

+ If you have an existing meditation practice, is there anything you'd like to add or change?
+ If you don't have a meditation practice, what are some resources you could explore to start one?
+ What are ways you can develop your intuition and find inspiration on a regular basis?

21

Building Confidence

Building confidence is often an issue for new and seasoned practitioners. I'll give you some concrete suggestions on ways to build your confidence: getting good training, dealing with the need for validation, and building a support network.

Practice makes perfect

As hypnosis and NLP teachers and practitioners, Sarah and Shawn Carson deal with confidence-building a lot with their clients and students, and offer some good recommendations:

"Get really good training! Having the surety of a great base, skill-wise, from which to begin is vitally important. Taking trainings that have plenty of real-life, hands-on experience will help give you the confidence needed. This gives the new practitioner a fully rounded tool kit upon which to draw.

"Having a training that offers continued support is important, too. Remember that you don't have to take every client who calls you; take time either by phone or in person to have a free consultation to ensure that you and the client are a good fit and refer out if you feel that you aren't skilled enough to help the prospective client.

"And remember, we're always learning—keep taking trainings, keep an open mind, and be curious. Then join a good practice group to hone your skills (or form one with your fellow students).

"Practice, practice, practice."

Sarah and Shawn are right—having a solid foundation of training is indispensable. In addition to your training, giving free sessions before you start charging and working professionally will help you build your confidence. You might do this by giving sessions to friends and family, or consider working in a clinic setting with mentoring support. This way you'll gain confidence as you encounter a range of physical, mental, and emotional issues, working with various situations and challenges presented by the people you're working with. You'll also be able to see measureable results over time.

Continuing education is another way to build confidence as you go deeper into the modality (modalities) you practice. I love learning new tools and refining foundational skills as I go deeper into my practice. There's always more to learn and in addition to building confidence, this can help keep your work fresh and expansive.

Getting comfortable not knowing

Once you have a solid foundation of training and hours of practice sessions under your belt, you can focus on relaxing into your work. Melissa Tiers puts it this way:

"One of the constant themes running through my classes is the idea of 'getting comfortable with not knowing.' If I had owned this idea years ago, I could have saved so much time, energy, and money. I would have relaxed into curiosity and invited my clients to join me there, with the burden of being the expert nowhere in sight.

"Whenever I do a demo for my students, I'm always pointing out the fact that I have no idea what I'm doing. And it's okay. In fact, it's more than okay; it's the way I want it to be. It keeps me flexible and open to all the surprises that happen in this mind field we play in.

"I don't know what I'm going to say until the client says something. I don't know what processes we will do until I hear how they talk about the issue and see how they gesture or look. The client is the expert on their particular problem because everyone has their own way of doing even the simplest of fears, limitations, and procrastinations. I think a big part of our job is to help them find their own solutions.

"For example, I recently had a client come into my office who said his anger was like a tight fist in his gut. I asked him to allow his mind to drop right down into that fist, and I asked him what has to happen in order to let it go? He said he needed to pry his father's hand off his fist because he was the one keeping it there. I asked him what would be the best way for him to do that, and he said he had to kiss the fingers and let them loosen up and go. His father didn't need to make him tough anymore. He did his job.

"I had him drop into trance and told him to allow that to happen. I sat back and watched as this tough man started to cry and his face showed me all the different emotions he was going through. I told him to allow his eyes to open only when he felt complete with this.

"Five minutes later, he emerged, grabbed my hand and thanked me and said it was done. He told me he had never felt so at peace. He insisted on paying me the full amount even though the whole session was less than fifteen minutes. An email two weeks later let me know he was continuing to feel more and more at ease and hadn't had an anger flare-up since.

"This is just one example of letting the client do the work. I couldn't have prepared for that session in any way, except to trust in his unconscious mind's abilities to give him what he needed. I never would have come up with kissing his father's fingers away. That much I do know."

Neediness and validation

The biggest thing I wish I knew when I was starting my practice was how to soften my need for validation. In other words, to let go of being needy! Even though we're practitioners, we're also human beings, and being needy is part of human nature. So instead of seeking support and validation from your clients, which is simply misdirected, I think we need to seek this love and support from our colleagues, mentors, friends, and family.

I think this is something that comes with experience, practice, and working on yourself and your issues. I've gotten so much better, but it's still hard not to base my worth as a practitioner solely on the feedback I get from clients. And to clarify, I'm not saying you shouldn't be looking for results—you do want to measure the effects and benefits of the sessions and the work that you do, but relying on it to validate your worth is something entirely different.

Similarly, Maria Rodriguez talks about it this way:

"I don't do this anymore—but I used to think of my clients as my friends, and they aren't. And this really hit a button of mine; when a client wasn't responding verbally during or after the session, I had the concern of 'am I doing a good job?'

"If you've received solid training, done the study, and you have the intuitive ability, just because the person doesn't respond by verbally telling you how amazing the session was, this doesn't necessarily mean you're not doing a good job. They might be digesting the information from the session, they might not want to hear or feel what you're helping them access about themselves, or you might not be a good fit for them as a practitioner. There are many possibilities, and it doesn't really matter.

"I think if you're doing this kind of work, you can't expect validation. People need to process, and I think it takes time for people to process, and it takes time for you to be comfortable in what you do.

"I'm going to do things to the best of my ability: do my homework, get everything done, and then what the client perceives you to do—it almost doesn't matter. Sometimes people want to hear what they want to hear. But it's not necessarily what you can give them, because it's something that they need to work on."

It's important to remember that we're not healing our clients. We're helping them heal themselves, offering them guidance and support through the work that we do, but the healing is in their hands.

I'm so glad I first got into this work through Reiki, and have had the teachers I've had. Reiki is such a great practice because you're taught from the beginning: if the client experiences healing, you didn't do it. And vice versa—if the client didn't receive the healing they wanted, or they had a negative feeling about it, you didn't do it. They're in charge of their own healing, taking the Reiki energy (or Ki) that they need; I'm not deciding for them.

Furthermore, it's important to remember that healing doesn't always happen in the way that we expect. Healing doesn't mean that you're necessarily cured. One particular client comes to mind. She came for help with knee pain, and while the knee pain didn't entirely diminish, she felt much more peaceful as a result of the sessions. She normally experienced a lot of anxiety, so this new feeling of peacefulness was huge for her.

Neediness isn't a bad thing. It's an important part of being human. We all have the need for connection and support. But looking to your clients for validation to fill this neediness is misplaced. There's a difference between validation of your work, and validation of you as a person! Having a strong spiritual practice or meditation is key to keeping this need in balance.

Developing a support network

In addition to having a meditation practice, developing a strong support network is another way to help you increase your confidence as a practitioner, and avoid seeking personal validation from your clients. Your support network can consist of many different kinds of people. My network consists of other practitioners, teachers, and mentors, as well as friends and family I can reach out to. Instead of being needy with my clients, I have more appropriate people to look to for support.

Having your own wellness practice can be isolating—seeing clients one-on-one each day—and developing a support network is a good way to balance this. For the first few years of my practice, I didn't realize how much this isolation affected me. Now I've learned over time how indispensible it is for me to connect with my support network after time spent alone with clients.

I found it especially reassuring to talk with other practitioners and discover that they had experienced situations and challenges similar to what I was going through. This encouraged me to understand that my feelings were valid, and hearing how other practitioners dealt with a particular challenge offered me additional resources to consider. I also felt less isolated.

I like being in a shared office suite. Even if I'm not interacting with other people in the office, being around them gives me a sense of community. I also set up a bimonthly call with a friend and colleague of mine to check in, share challenges and achievements, vent, and get advice. I meet in person for lunch periodically with another friend and fellow practitioner.

As I mentioned earlier, getting sessions from fellow practitioners and mentors is another huge support for me. It helps me work through things that come up in my life (which often relate to issues similar to those my clients are coming to me with—you've probably noticed this in your own work). And I'm in this work because getting sessions has been so helpful for me in my own life—kind of meta, I know!

Other people find it helpful to join a practice group, trade sessions with another practitioner, attend conferences or participate in associations for your modality, or use online resources such as Facebook or LinkedIn groups for practitioners in their field.

These are all ways to build a professional network with your peers and mentors. In addition to gaining the support you need, you'll also have additional resources to offer your clients when they need referrals to other types of practitioners. Ideally, your professional support network can also refer their clients to you as appropriate.

Homework: Building your support network

Think about your existing resources and support system.

+ Write down three ways you can fulfill your need for connection and support besides positive client feedback.
+ If you don't have a support network in place, what kind of support do you need? What can you do to build it?

22

Top Tips From Me
(& Other Successful Practitioners):
What We Wish We'd Known

I've covered a lot of steps to help you build a successful practice doing the work you love—from finding office space to crafting your pitch and marketing to your niche, from building and maintaining your client base to setting up financial systems, from building your confidence to taking care of yourself along the way. You now have a solid template to help you get your practice set up and moving in the right direction.

I've saved the best for last—I gathered top tips and advice from the seasoned practitioners interviewed throughout this book to help you implement all of the above. I asked each of the practitioners I interviewed for this book to give me their top recommendations—what they wish they knew starting out.

Reiki teacher and practitioner Frans Stiene:

"I think there are three important elements a new practitioner needs to remember and they are interlinked with each other. The first is to meditate, developing a solid foundation. Ask your teacher to guide you with a solid meditation practice, if you don't already have one, so you can become a clear vehicle for helping others.

"The second is to let go of your attachment to a certain outcome for your client. This attachment can be a pitfall, because if the outcome doesn't happen, we get angry with the practice, the system, and/or with ourselves, or even the client. So step away from hoping for something to take place: your hope that your client feels something, your hope that your client is healed, your hope . . . fill in the blank here.

"Hope is a big stumbling block, but we can overcome this through our daily meditation practice, because hope is in essence based on fear: that my client doesn't feel anything, that my client doesn't get healed, etc.

"The third element is to refrain from interpreting and labeling what is happening. When we label things we start to stick them in a box: when things are in a box they are not as open as the universe. The universe itself is not labeling anything, so let go of labeling: labeling of what feels hot, cold, tingling, pulsating, you name it.

"We label because we feel insecure; we need to hold onto something, but again, through our own personal meditation practice we start to let go of our insecurity and become as open as the universe in which there is no need to label or interpret."

Polarity teacher and practitioner Gary Strauss:

"I still feel good about doing sessions. I started working professionally in 1980, and I love it after all these years. That's how you want to be as a practitioner.

"Getting a session a week is a way to deal with your creative expressions. Be curious, don't come to any answers, be neutral.

"Take your time: one session at a time. Each time you do a session it's like going to the gym and working out—you're always trying to get it right. On the one hand, if you're coming from the right place it's always right. On the other hand, it's okay not to get it—we probably never really get it right anyway—something else is at work here, and having good manners, boundaries, and slowly developing your skills over time will get you there.

"You should have the mind-set to be everything to your client, and nothing to your client at the same time.

"You have to earn the trust and the power of being able to do this work, and you do this every time you do a session, every class you take, all the time and money it takes educating and developing yourself and your life. It takes a lifetime of commitment to become really good at this work."

Thai massage therapist and coach Pamela Herrick:

"My younger self had absolutely no idea how much personal growth, on an intellectual, spiritual, energetic and physical level, would come from being a Thai massage therapist. My work has fundamentally changed who I am, and I am incredibly grateful for that.

"My advice to new practitioners is to be hungry for knowledge and to be completely client-focused in your work. From this, you can build an amazing and rewarding life-long practice."

Integrative hypnosis practitioner and trainer Melissa Tiers:

"I love giving up the idea that I have to be the expert. Change work is a dance—a fluid, ever-changing interaction that's full of possibilities. When you allow your client to show you the steps, the pace and lead seem effortless. Most of our clients' issues (and our own) stem from the need to be in control and our search for certainty in an uncertain world.

"So give it up. Let go of the need to be right. Let go of the idea of finding the perfect script or training that will make you feel like an authority on the subject. Make friends with uncertainty and get comfortable with not knowing 'the best' way to fix it all and your sessions will flow very differently. Of that you can be certain."

Reiki teacher and practitioner Joanna Crespo:

"Have fun. Take care of yourself. Respect the sessions.

"I thought I might have more to say, but then realized that everything is in one's journey of learning and refining."

* * *

Astrology coach and spiritual counselor Maria Rodriguez:

"Here's what I would recommend to new practitioners: 1. Make sure that you have the proper credentials for your field. 2. Remember that marketing your business is very important. 3. Find ways to have clients repeat the service. 4. Email clients periodically and offer some kind of incentive like a coupon or gift for referrals."

NLP and hypnosis teachers and practitioners Sarah and Shawn Carson:

"Remember that you have all the resources you need to change. And you know the rest . . . at least unconsciously!"

My top recommendation would be to be gentle with yourself. Building your practice and the administrative components that go with it take longer than you probably think they will or should. Get sessions regularly from practitioners who can serve as mentors to you so you can work through your own stuff. And then sit with this stuff in your meditation practice.

And most of all, enjoy the journey along the way. The fact that you have this amazing opportunity to help people who need it, helping them grow and change and expand in their lives, is an amazing gift!

Appendix

Bonuses

The Business Starter Kit on my website (www.centertruehealth.com/business-starter-kit) includes real-world templates you can use for managing your clients, building an email list, and keeping track of income and expenses. You'll also find useful resources for setting up your business, as well as information on the practitioners and teachers interviewed in this book.

The Business Starter Kit includes:

+ Sample weekly and monthly administrative checklist
+ Sample Excel templates for:
    + Budgeting income and expenses
    + Client tracking
    + Gift certificates
    + Quarterly taxes
+ Sample Intake Form
+ How to figure out your session fees and annual income

About the Author

Deborah Flanagan established the Center for True Health in NYC in 2008 and has since guided thousands of people through major life changes, helping them find true health and balance using Reiki, hypnosis, and reflexology. Her unique approach has been featured on *The Dr. Oz Show* and in *O, the Oprah Magazine*; she also teaches Reiki and sees patients at NYU Langone Medical Center, and previously at Beth Israel Medical Center. She is a certified hypnotist through the National Guild of Hypnotists, and is a certified reflexologist through the American Reflexology Certification Board and a member of the Reflexology Association of America and the New York State Reflexology Association. Deborah completed a 600-hour Reiki training through the New York Open Center, continues to study with Frans Stiene at the International House of Reiki, and practices Reiki meditation and self-care daily.

Prior to embarking on her wellness career, Deborah garnered more than fifteen years of leadership experience in the nonprofit sector as the director of development for distinguished arts organizations including the Paul Taylor Dance Company, the American Symphony Orchestra League, and the Academy of American Poets. An award-winning poet and the author of *Or, Gone* (Tupelo Press, 2015), Deborah's work has been published in *AGNI*, *The Gettysburg Review*, *Ploughshares*, *FIELD*, and *The Southern Review*. She is also a former professional ballet dancer, having toured with Southern Ballet Theatre and taught ballet to at-risk children. Her poetry and dance background enables her to bring to her wellness practice an intimate knowledge of the language and silence of the body, and she thinks of her current work as a union of matter and spirit.

To learn more about Deborah's work, go to centertruehealth.com, where you can sign up for her monthly newsletter and get tips to help you find more balance in your life.